Practical Paint.NET

The Powerful No-Cost Image Editor for Microsoft Windows

Phillip Whitt

Apress®

Practical Paint.NET: The Powerful No-Cost Image Editor for Microsoft Windows

Phillip Whitt
Columbus, GA, USA

ISBN-13 (pbk): 978-1-4842-7282-4
https://doi.org/10.1007/978-1-4842-7283-1

ISBN-13 (electronic): 978-1-4842-7283-1

Managing Director, Apress Media LLC: Welmoed Spahr
Acquisitions Editor: Susan McDermott
Development Editor: James Markham
Coordinating Editor: Jessica Vakili

Distributed to the book trade worldwide by Springer Science+Business Media New York, 1 NY Plaza, New York, NY 10004. Phone 1-800-SPRINGER, fax (201) 348-4505, e-mail orders-ny@ springer-sbm.com, or visit www.springeronline.com. Apress Media, LLC is a California LLC and the sole member (owner) is Springer Science + Business Media Finance Inc (SSBM Finance Inc). SSBM Finance Inc is a **Delaware** corporation.

For information on translations, please e-mail booktranslations@springernature.com; for reprint, paperback, or audio rights, please e-mail bookpermissions@springernature.com.

Apress titles may be purchased in bulk for academic, corporate, or promotional use. eBook versions and licenses are also available for most titles. For more information, reference our Print and eBook Bulk Sales web page at http://www.apress.com/bulk-sales.

Any source code or other supplementary material referenced by the author in this book is available to readers on GitHub via the book's product page, located at www.apress.com/978-1-4842-7282-4. For more detailed information, please visit http://www.apress.com/source-code.

Printed on acid-free paper

*This book is dedicated to my family and friends;
they are always incredibly supportive and encouraging
in my writing endeavors.*

Table of Contents

About the Author

Phillip Whitt has been involved in image creation and editing since the 1990s. He has been a digital photo retoucher and restoration professional since 2000 and has digitally enhanced and repaired countless photographs since then. Mr. Whitt has been an author since 2014 and contributed several books to the Apress library including *Beginning Pixlr Editor* and *Practical Glimpse.*

About the Technical Reviewer

 **Massimo Nardone** has more than 22 years of experience in security, web/mobile development, cloud, and IT architecture. His true IT passions are security and Android.

He has been programming and teaching how to program with Android, Perl, PHP, Java, VB, Python, C/C++, and MySQL for more than 20 years.

He holds a Master of Science degree in Computing Science from the University of Salerno, Italy.

He has worked as a project manager, software engineer, research engineer, chief security architect, information security manager, PCI/SCADA auditor, and senior lead IT security/cloud/SCADA architect for many years.

Acknowledgments

I would like to acknowledge the professionals at Apress Publishing, whose assistance and guidance are always very much appreciated.

Introduction

There was a time when digital image editing was a specialty that only trained professionals were capable of performing. Over the years, more and more software programs became available for both professionals and nonprofessionals. Adobe Photoshop has long been the industry standard in professional graphic design and photography, but it has a very steep learning curve and can be daunting for beginners. The open source program GIMP (GNU Image Manipulation Program) is free and almost as powerful as Photoshop. Many freelance professionals and advanced amateurs use GIMP, but like Photoshop, it also has a steep learning curve.

Paint.NET—Quite Possibly the Perfect Solution

For those with little or no image editing experience, Photoshop and GIMP may be too overwhelming. Over the years, I've had many clients tell me they made an attempt at learning image editing, only to get discouraged by the complexity of either Photoshop or GIMP. Additionally, these programs usually have more features than the casual user really needs.

Paint.NET is a sleek but powerful program for Windows that might be just the ticket. It's free to download and use (although there is a paid version for a nominal fee that helps with development costs—more about that in Chapter 1). Even though it's not in the same league as Photoshop or GIMP, it is a capable image editing program for nonprofessionals.

Paint.NET can be useful to small business owners, aspiring photographers, genealogists, or anyone with a need for a general-purpose editing program that can handle basic photo-editing tasks or graphics creation. It offers a good assortment of tools and features that allows the user to tackle a variety of editing tasks. The capabilities of Paint.NET can be expanded by installing third-party *plugins*. We'll look closer at that in Chapter 1.

Paint.NET can be especially useful to art educators in the realm of public education. School budget concerns are common, and they usually seem to impact art and music departments the hardest. When paying for a subscription to use Photoshop isn't an option, here are some reasons to consider incorporating Paint.NET into an art curriculum:

- It's free to download and use.

- It can be used for personal, academic, government, and commercial purposes.

- It can be installed on as many computers (it only works on Windows) as you like—the Paint.NET license can be accessed here: `www.getpaint.net/license.html`.

- The interface is uncluttered and easy to learn.

- It's a great starter program for students learning digital imaging; most of the skills learned using Paint.NET are transferable to more complex programs like Photoshop or GIMP.

Figure 1 shows the Paint.NET interface.

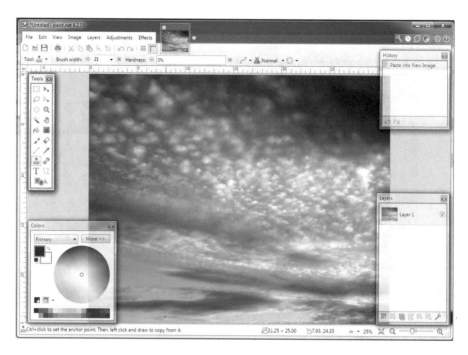

Figure 1. *The default Paint.NET interface*

What Can Paint.NET Do?

Even though (comparatively speaking) Paint.NET is a lightweight program, it can be used to achieve impressive results. It can be used to edit digital photos, such as exposure and color correction, restoration, and retouching. Figure 2 shows a before and after comparison of an image with the power lines digitally removed (this lesson appears in Chapter 6).

Figure 2. *This example shows the power lines removed using Paint.NET*

Paint.NET can also be used to create original raster (bitmapped) artwork. The illustration (Figure 3) is an example of one I created in Paint.NET in 2019.

Figure 3. *This illustration was created using Paint.NET*

Paint.NET offers a few artistic effects to turn photos into digital art. Figure 4 shows a before and after example of a photo turned into a digital pen-and-ink drawing using the *Ink Sketch Artistic Effect*.

Figure 4. *A before and after comparison showing the original photo and the image after Ink Sketch Artistic Effect*

What You'll Learn from This Book

If you're new to image editing, you'll establish a good foundation after you've completed the tutorials. You'll have gained some valuable experience and learn the following:

- The Paint.NET interface

- How to install the BoltBait Plugin Pack to further expand the program's capabilities (you'll learn about other plugins available for Paint.NET in the Appendix)

- The Paint.NET tools

- How layers work

- How to make tonal and color adjustments

- How to modify, retouch, and restore photos

- How to make composites (such as add elements or change a background)

- How to create digital art (both from scratch and using artistic effects on photos)

If you're now ready to dive in and start learning this handy program, let's move on to Chapter 1.

CHAPTER 1

An Overview of Paint.NET

Now that you've been introduced to Paint.NET, we'll cover the steps required to acquire and install the program. Then we'll start our general overview of Paint.NET.

The topics covered in this chapter are

- System Requirements

- Acquiring and Installing Paint.NET

- The Main Window

- Menus

- The Settings Dialog

- The Color Scheme

- Supported File Formats

- Installing BoltBait's Plugin Pack

- Chapter Conclusion

© Phillip Whitt 2022
P. Whitt, *Practical Paint.NET*, https://doi.org/10.1007/978-1-4842-7283-1_1

System Requirements

Paint.NET works on Windows systems with these specifications (these are the minimum requirements):

- Windows 10 (version 1607 "Anniversary Update" or newer)

- Windows 8.1

- 1GHz processor (dual-core recommended)

- 1GB of RAM

Note   Paint.NET requires Microsoft's .NET Framework 4.7.2 to work—if it's not on your system, it will be automatically installed during the Paint.NET installation process.

Acquiring and Installing Paint.NET

We'll now proceed to the official website to download the program:

1. Go to the Paint.NET website at `www.getpaint.net`— you'll then be taken to the home page. I recommend reading it over before proceeding to the download page.

2. When you are ready to download the program, just click the *Download* button *or* the link as indicated in Figure 1-1.

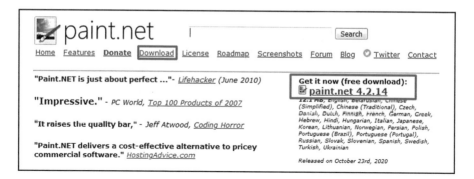

Figure 1-1. *To proceed to the download page, click either the Download button or the link indicated*

Note   Step 2 navigates to a page that offers two options—one is for the *Store* (paid) version of Paint.NET, and the other for the *Classic* (free) version. The main difference is the paid version is automatically updated. The paid version (which is only about seven US dollars) also helps with the ongoing development costs of Paint.NET. If you opt for the paid version of Paint.NET, the installation process will be automatic.

---

3. Scroll to the bottom of the page to find two options for acquiring Paint.NET; one is paid (Store version) and one is free (Classic version) (Figure 1-2).

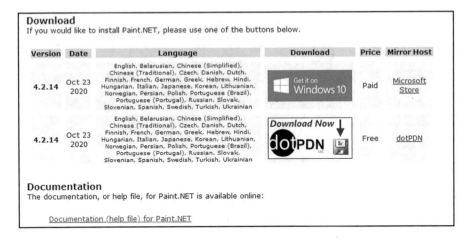

Figure 1-2. *The download options for either the Store or the Classic version of Paint.NET*

4. Clicking the link for the free version navigates to the page shown in Figure 1-3. Click the link to download the installer package.

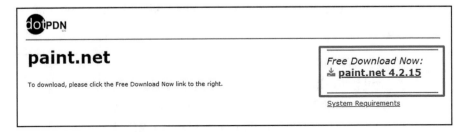

Figure 1-3. *The link to download the free (Classic) version of Paint.NET*

5. The installer package should be located in the Downloads folder (Figure 1-4).

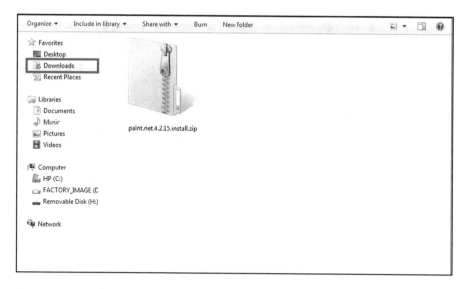

Figure 1-4. *The installer zip file package should be located in the Downloads folder*

6.   Double-click the zip file to open it, then double-click the *paint.net4.2.15.exe* file.

7.   If the Windows Account Control dialog (Figure 1-5) opens asking for permission to make changes to your system, click *Yes* to proceed.

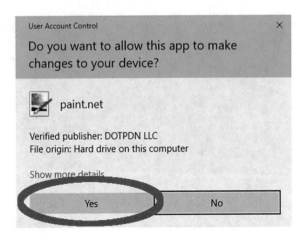

Figure 1-5. *Click the Yes to button to proceed*

8. The installation process will commence; a dialog
    window (Figure 1-6) displays offering the option of
    Express or Custom installation; it's recommended
    that most users choose *Express*.

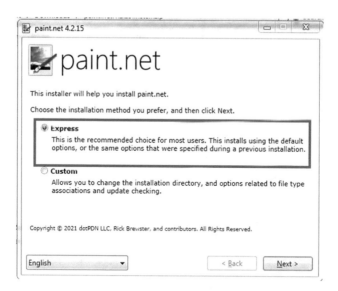

Figure 1-6. *Most users should choose the Express installation option*

9. A dialog window (Figure 1-7) containing the License Agreement is displayed; it's recommended you read the terms—if you agree with the terms, click the *I Agree* button, then *Next* to install Paint.NET.

Figure 1-7. *Click the I Agree option and then the Next button to complete the installation*

The Main Window

When Paint.NET is first launched, the user interface or the *Main Window* appears. It bears resemblance to other image editing programs, but you may notice it has a slimmer, less cluttered appearance.

The Main Window is divided into ten sections as shown in Figure 1-8.

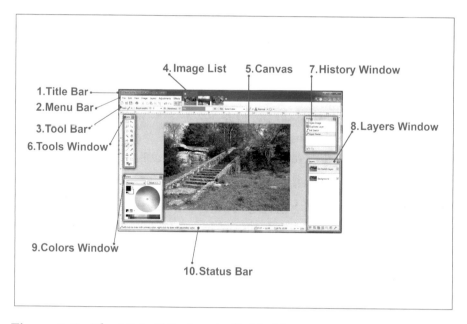

Figure 1-8. *The Main Window is divided into ten sections*

Let's take a brief look at each of these sections and their purpose:

1. **Title Bar**—Displays the name of the open image; it will be named Untitled by default if the document hasn't been given a name. It also displays the program's version number.

2. **Menu Bar**—Contains seven menus on the left (such as *New, Open, Save,* etc.) and six utility icons on the right.

3. **Tool Bar**—Not to be confused with the *Tools Window*, the Tool Bar is just below the Menu Bar, where the active tool and its parameters are displayed.

4. **Image List**—Each image that is open in Paint.NET displays a preview thumbnail. Clicking a thumbnail makes the image active.

5. **Canvas**—The area where the active image is displayed and editing actions (such as drawing, painting, selecting, etc.) take place. The Canvas along with the gray surrounding area is collectively called the Editing Window.

6. **Tools Window**—This is a floating window that displays the tool icons. The active tool is highlighted in the Tools Window. A "tool tip" is displayed when the pointer is hovered over a tool icon.

7. **History Window**—This window displays every action that has been performed within the current editing session; this enables you to revert to an earlier point in the editing history. You can toggle back and forth through the steps in the History Window. Using *Undo* or *Redo* toggles backward or forward. Closing the image or Paint.NET clears the history completely.

8. **Layers Window**—This window displays thumbnail previews of the layers comprising the active image. Layers are managed from this window; new layers can be added, layers deleted, moved, or edited. Double-clicking a layer preview thumbnail opens the *Layer Properties* dialog.

9. **Colors Window**—This window is for selecting and managing colors; the window can be expanded to display more options by clicking the *More* button. It can be collapsed to its original state by clicking *Less*.

10. **Status Bar**—On the left half, it displays brief
    information about the active tool. On the right half,
    it displays the image size, cursor coordinates, and
    units of measurement.

The smaller windows (Tools, History, Layers, and Colors) "float,"
meaning they can be moved and arranged as needed by clicking and
dragging into place. Their visibility can be toggled on or off by clicking the
tabs in the upper-right area of the Main Window (Figure 1-9). Also located
near these options are *Settings* and *Help* tabs.

Note   For the purpose of uniformity, the ten parts of the Main
Window described earlier essentially follow the conventions used in
the Paint.NET documentation.

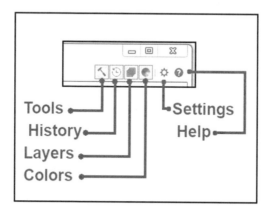

Figure 1-9. *The Windows Tabs, Settings, and Help*

Menus

The menus are located along the Menu Bar and provide a variety of commands for working with your image:

- **The File Menu**—Like most image editing programs, the File Menu contains commands to open, acquire, close, save, and print images. The commands in the File Menu are

  - **New (Ctrl+N)**—This creates a single layered blank image filled with white. By default, the canvas size is 800 pixels X 600 pixels at 96 DPI, or the size of the image contained in the clipboard.

  - **Open (Ctrl+O)**—This command opens an existing image for editing.

  - **Open Recent**—Opens a sub-menu that allows access to the last ten images opened with Paint. NET.

  - **Acquire**—This opens a sub-menu that allows a new image to be imported from a scanner or digital camera connected to the computer.

  - **Save (Ctrl+S)**—Saves the image with the current filename. If the image has not been previously saved, or if the file type specified requires configuration (such as a JPEG file), the Save Configuration dialog is displayed. If the image is untitled, assigning a name to it will be required before it will be saved.

- **Save As (Ctrl+Shift+S)**—Allows a new name, format, location, and settings to be applied to the saved image. This allows you to save a copy of an edited image while maintaining and retaining the original, unaltered image.

- **Save All (Ctrl+Alt+S)**—Saves each image that has been edited since it was opened. When possible, the existing filename, path, format, and settings will be reused to overwrite the existing image.

- **Print (Ctrl+P)**—Opens the Windows Photo Printing interface; the image can then be sent to a connected printer.

- **Close (Ctrl+W)**—This command closes the current image; when there are unsaved changes, you'll be prompted to confirm before the closure proceeds.

- **Exit**—This closes the Paint.NET program; if you've made unsaved changes, you'll be prompted to save the changes to the image before the application closes.

- **The Edit Menu**—Contains commands such as Undo, Redo, Copy, and Paste. The commands in the Edit Menu are

  - **Undo (Ctrl+Z)**—Undoes the most recent editing action performed on the image.

  - **Redo (Ctrl+Y)**—Reverses the most recent action that has been undone.

  - **Cut (Ctrl+X)**—Removes a selected area of the active layer and stores it on the clipboard.

- **Copy (Ctrl+C)**—Copies a selected area of the active layer and stores it on the clipboard.

- **Copy Merged (Ctrl+Shift+C)**—Copies all the layers to the clipboard without using the Flatten command.

- **Paste (Ctrl+V)**—Pastes the contents of the clipboard onto an active layer.

- **Paste into New Layer (Ctrl+Shift+V)**—Creates a new layer, then pastes the contents of the clipboard in it.

- **Paste into New Image (Ctrl+Alt+V)**—Creates a new image, then pastes the contents of the clipboard in it.

- **Copy Selection (Ctrl+Alt+Shift+C)**—Copies the dimensions of a selection to the clipboard; the selection shape can be applied to another layer.

- **Paste Selection (Ctrl+Alt+Shift+V)**—Reconstructs the shape of a copied selection on an active layer; uses the *Replace* selection mode by default.

- **Erase Selection (Delete key)**—Removes the pixels from the selected area of the active layer.

- **Fill Selection (Backspace key)**—Fills a selected area with the Primary Color.

- **Invert Selection (Ctrl+I)**—Inverts the selection; the area inside the selection is now deselected, while the area outside is selected.

- **Select All (Ctrl+A)**—Selects the entire active layer.

- **Deselect (Ctrl+D)**—Deactivates the selection(s) in an active layer.

- **The View Menu**—Contains commands that change the way the image or workspace is displayed. The image isn't altered, only the way it's viewed:

  - **Zoom in**—Magnifies the image; zooms in fixed steps from 100% through 6400%.

  - **Zoom out**—Reduces the size of the image.

  - **Zoom to Window**—Zooms the image to the limits of the editing window or to full size.

  - **Zoom to Selection**—Increases the view size of any active selection until the bounding rectangle reaches the limit of the viewable area.

  - **Actual Size**—Sets the zoom level at 100%.

  - **Pixel Grid**—Overlays the current image with a grid with each cell being 1 pixel in size.

  - **Rulers**—Displays or hides the rulers at the top and along the left edge of the image canvas.

  - **Pixels**—Sets the unit of measurement to pixels.

  - **Inches**—Sets the unit of measurement to inches.

  - **Centimeters**—Sets the unit of measurement to centimeters.

- **The Image Menu**—Contains commands that affect all the layers in the current image:

  - **Crop to Selection**—Trims the current image down to the size of a selection; the resulting crop will be either square or rectangular, depending on the proportions (and regardless of the shape) of the selection.

- **Resize**—Changes the size of the current image.

- **Canvas Size**—Enlarges or shrinks the canvas without affecting the size of the image on it.

- **Flip Horizontal/Flip Vertical**—These commands rotate the image (including all layers) horizontally or vertically.

- **Rotate 90° Clockwise/Rotate 90° Counter-Clockwise/Rotate 180°**—These commands rotate the image by 90° (in either clockwise or counter-clockwise directions) or by 180°.

- **Flatten**—Merges all the layers in an image into a single layer.

- **The Layers Menu**—Contains commands that affect the layers in the current image:

  - **Add New Layer**—Adds a new transparent layer to the current image above the active layer.

  - **Delete Layer**—Deletes the active layer from the image.

  - **Duplicate Layer**—Makes a copy of the active layer.

  - **Merge Layer Down**—Merges the active layer onto the one directly below, combining them into one layer.

  - **Import From File**—Opens one (or more) image file to be imported as a layer (or layers) into the active image.

- **Flip Layer Horizontally/Flip Layer Vertically**—
  These commands flip the active layer horizontally
  (creating a mirrored view or vice versa) and vertically
  (creating an upside down view or vice versa).

- **Rotate 180°**—Rotates the active layer 180°.

- **Rotate/Zoom**—Opens a dialog window that allows
  the active layer to be rotated, panned, and enlarged
  or reduced.

- **Go to Top Layer**—Makes the topmost layer active.

- **Go to Layer Above**—Navigates from the current
  layer to the one directly above.

- **Go to Layer Below**—Makes the next layer below
  the layer active.

- **Go to Bottom Layer**—Makes the bottommost layer
  active.

- **Move Layer to Top**—Moves the active layer to the
  top of the layer stack.

- **Move Layer Up**—Moves the active layer up one level.

- **Move Layer Down**—Moves the active layer down
  one level.

- **Move Layer to Bottom**—Moves the active layer to
  the bottom of the layer stack.

- **Layer Properties (F4 Key)**—Opens the Properties
  dialog for the active layer; this allows you to change
  the layer name, as well as set layer visibility, blend
  mode, and opacity.

- **The Adjustments Menu**—Affects the color and/or tone in the active image:

Note   Some of the Adjustments mentioned are third-party plugins from the BoltBait website; we'll cover installing the Plugin Pack a little later in this chapter.

- **Auto-Level (Ctrl+Shift+L)**—A nonconfigurable operation that equalizes the colors in an image and equalizes the tone in black and white images.

- **Black and White (Ctrl+Shift+G)**—A nonconfigurable operation that removes the colors from an image; the image is now represented in black, white, and shades of gray.

- **Black and White (BoltBait Plugin)**—This basically does the same thing as the previous operation, but opens a Brightness/Contrast dialog; *this command isn't available unless BoltBait's Plugin Pack is installed.*

- **Brightness/Contrast**—Increases or decreases the brightness and/or contrast in an image.

- **Color Balance (BoltBait Plugin)**—Adjusts the balance of a color in an image by shifting from one color to its opposite on the color wheel; *this command is unavailable unless BoltBait's Plugin Pack is installed.*

- **Combined Adjustments (BoltBait Plugin)**—Combines the Brightness/Contrast, Hue/Saturation/Lightness, and Color Conversion commands in one dialog window. *This command is unavailable unless BoltBait's Plugin Pack is installed.*

- **Curves (Ctrl+Shift+M)**—Curves is used to adjust the tone (highlights, midtones, and shadows) and color; it can be used on the composite image or each RGB channel.

- **Hue/Saturation (Ctrl+Shift+U)**—Adjusts the hue, saturation, and lightness in an image.

- **Hue/Saturation (BoltBait Plugin)**—Performs the same operations as the previous dialog, but with additional functions; *this command is unavailable unless BoltBait's Plugin Pack is installed.*

- **Invert Colors (Ctrl+Shift+I)**—Swaps each color with its opposite on the color wheel, resulting in an effect similar to a photographic negative.

- **Levels (Ctrl+L)**—This dialog is used to adjust the tone (highlights, midtones, and shadows) and color; it can be used on the composite image or each RGB channel. It's used to achieve similar results as Curves.

- **Posterize (Ctrl+Shift+P)**—This dialog is used to reduce the gradual transition of color and tone, resulting in more solid colors, giving the image a retro or posterized appearance. It works with the RGB channels linked or each channel individually.

- **Sepia (Ctrl+Shift+E)**—Removes the colors in an image and creates an aged sepia look with reddish-brownish tones.

- **The Effects Menu**—The Effects Menu contains sub-menus; these contain operations to apply effects to photographic images:

Note   Because there are so many different effects, an in-depth coverage would result in an unnecessarily long chapter. They'll be touched on briefly here. Some of them will be used in later tutorials, and you can find more in-depth information in the Paint. NET documentation: `www.getpaint.net/doc/latest/ EffectsMenu.html`.

- **Artistic**—As shown in Figure 1-10, this menu contains a set of sub-menus with several artistic effects: Dream, Ink Sketch, Oil Painting, Oil Painting +, Pastel, and Pencil Sketch. *Plugins are indicated by a puzzle piece–shaped icon and are only available after BoltBait's Plugin Pack has been installed.*

Figure 1-10. *The Artistic menu and sub-menu*

- **Blurs**—This menu contains a set of sub-menus
  (Figure 1-11) with several blur effects: Fragment,
  Gaussian Blur, Gaussian Blur +, Motion Blur, Radial
  Blur, Surface Blur, Unfocus, and Zoom Blur. *Plugins
  are indicated by a puzzle piece–shaped icon and are
  only available after BoltBait's Plugin Pack has been
  installed.*

Figure 1-11. *The Blurs menu and sub-menu*

- **Distort**—This menu contains a set of sub-
  menus (Figure 1-12) with a number of effects for
  creating various distortions: Bulge, Crystalize,
  Dents, Frosted Glass, Morphology, Pixelate, Polar
  Inversion, Tile Reflection, and Twist.

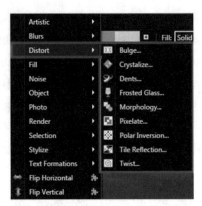

Figure 1-12. *The Distort menu and sub-menu*

- **Fill**—This menu contains two plugins (if installed): From Clipboard and From File. The From Clipboard command fills a selection with the contents of the clipboard, with several optional tiling effects available (Figure 1-13).

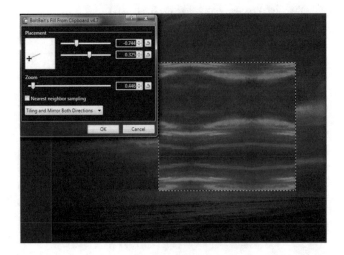

Figure 1-13. *The Fill From Clipboard dialog window*

The From File command fills an active layer with an imported image file with several optional tiling effects available (Figure 1-14). *This menu is only available after BoltBait's Plugin Pack has been installed.*

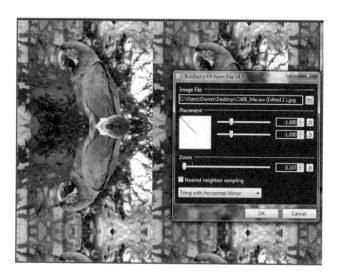

Figure 1-14. *The Fill From File dialog window*

- **Noise**—This menu contains a sub-menu of commands for adding, smoothing, and reducing noise: Add Noise, Median, and Reduce Noise (Figure 1-15).

Figure 1-15. *The Noise menu and sub-menu*

- **Object**—This menu contains a sub-menu of plugins (if installed) for adding effects to an object: Bevel Object, Feather Object, Inner Shadow, Object Shadow, Outline Object, Paste Alpha, Switch Alpha to Gray, and Switch Gray to Alpha (Figure 1-16). *This menu is only available after BoltBait's Plugin Pack has been installed.*

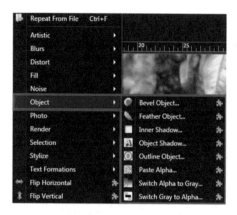

Figure 1-16. *The Object menu and sub-menu*

- **Photo**—This menu contains a long list of sub-menu commands for modifying and enhancing digital photos: Combined Adjustments, Glow, Level Horizon/Plumb Bob, Meme Maker, Red Eye Removal, Remove Dust, Seam Reducing-Reduce Height, Seam Carving-Reduce Width, Sharpen, Sharpen Landscape, Soften Portrait, Vignette, and Vignette + (Figure 1-17). *Plugins are indicated by a puzzle piece–shaped icon and are only available after BoltBait's Plugin Pack has been installed.*

Figure 1-17. *The Photo menu and sub-menu*

- **Render**—This menu (Figure 1-18) contains a list of sub-menu commands for creating patterns, colors, and objects: Calendar, Chart or Graph, Clouds, Dimensions, Flames, Gradient, Grid/Checkerboard, Julia Fractal, Mandelbrot Fractal, Polygon/Stars, and Turbulence. *Plugins are indicated by a puzzle piece–shaped icon and are only available after BoltBait's Plugin Pack has been installed.*

Figure 1-18. *The Render menu and sub-menu*

- **Selection**—This menu (Figure 1-19) contains a list of plugins for adding effects to selections: Bevel Selection, Bevel Selection Edge, Feather Selection, Inner Shadow, Outline Selection. *This menu is only available after BoltBait's Plugin Pack has been installed.*

Figure 1-19. *The Selection menu and sub-menu*

- **Stylize**—This menu (Figure 1-20) contains a list of commands that produce stylized changes to an original based on edge detection: Edge Detect, Emboss, Floyd-Steinberg Dithering, Outline, and Relief. *This menu is only available after BoltBait's Plugin Pack has been installed.*

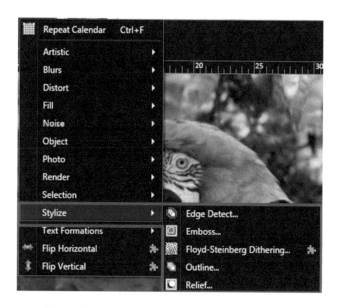

Figure 1-20. *The Stylize menu and sub-menu*

- **Text Formations**—This menu (Figure 1-21) contains
  two plugins for creating stylized text: Creative Text Pro
  and Outlined/Gradient text. *This menu is only available*
  after BoltBait's Plugin Pack has been installed.

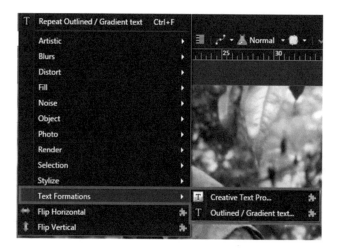

Figure 1-21. *The Text Formations menu and sub-menu*

- **Flip Horizontal/Flip Vertical**—These commands
  (Figure 1-22) flip the active layer horizontally or
  vertically. *These commands are only available after
  BoltBait's Plugin Pack has been installed.*

Figure 1-22. *The Flip Horizontal and Flip Vertical plugins*

The Settings Dialog

The Settings Dialog houses several configuration settings for Paint.NET
and is accessed by clicking the tab shown in Figure 1-23.

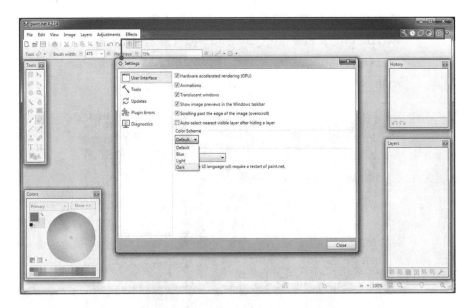

Figure 1-23. *The Settings Dialog contains several configuration
settings for Paint.NET*

The configurations that can be made from the Settings Dialog are

- **User Interface**—This tab presents options to configure how Paint.NET appears to the user.

- **Tools**—This tab allows the user to change the default settings and actions of the tools.

- **Updates**—This option checks for the latest updates/ newest version of Paint.NET.

- **Plugin Errors**—Checks for Paint.NET plugins that fail to load or function properly; the plugin filename and details of the error are displayed.

- **Diagnostics**—Displays information about the version of Paint.NET being used and the computer system. There is an option to copy the information to the clipboard to send to the developer and to access the *Crash Logs* folder for crash-related issues.

The Color Scheme

Paint.NET offers a few choices in the Color Scheme:

- Light/Default

- Blue

- Dark

The Color Scheme for Paint.NET can be changed from the Settings Dialog if desired. In Figure 1-24, the Color Scheme is to the *Dark* setting.

Figure 1-24. *The Dark setting in the Color Scheme*

Note   These days, most image editing and graphics creation programs utilize a dark color scheme—ostensibly to help reduce eyestrain during extensive editing sessions. I prefer using the dark color scheme, which is shown in the figures throughout the rest of this book. The color scheme you prefer to use is optional, and changing it is not required to follow the tutorials in later chapters.

Supported File Formats

Paint.NET supports several file formats, as shown in Table 1-1.

Table 1-1. *The File Formats That Paint.NET Supports*

Format	Extension(s)	Note
Paint.NET	.pdn	This is the application's proprietary file format; maintains the layers in a multi-layered image when saved.
PNG (Portable Network Graphics)	.png	Typically used for web graphics, this format compresses image data with little loss of quality; supports transparent backgrounds.
JPEG (Joint Photographic Experts Group)	.jpg, .jpeg, .jpe, .jfif, .exif	A commonly used file format, this is a lossy format that balances image compression and quality.
JPEG XR (JPEG Extended Range)	.jxr, .wdp, .wmp	Windows 8.1 and later required.
Bitmap	.bmp, .dib, .rle	A nondestructive file format; images are saved in high quality but large file sizes.
GIF	.gif	A common format for the Web, supports transparent backgrounds.
TGA (Targa)	.tga	
DirectDraw Surface	.dds	
TIFF (Tagged Image File Format)	.tif, .tiff	A widely used raster graphics file format used in the graphics industry.
HEIC	.heic	Windows 10 v1809 + required plus Microsoft HEVC Video Extensions.
WebP	.webp	Maximum image dimensions: 16383 x 16383.
AVI	.avif	

Installing BoltBait's Plugin Pack

One of the advantages of using Paint.NET is that it can be expanded by installing third-party *plugins*. You were introduced to some of them in the *Menus* section of this chapter.

Plugins add specific features to the program. On its own, Paint. NET offers basic image editing features, but adding plugins increases its capabilities. There are tons of useful plugins available, many of which will be covered in the Appendix of this book.

Some of the tutorials in this book require the use of some of the plugins that are in *BoltBait's Plugin Pack* (for expediency, it's recommended that you install everything when you come to that step).

Here are the steps to take to download and install BoltBait's Plugin Pack (Paint.NET must already be installed on your computer):

1. Go to the official BoltBait website: `www.boltbait. com/pdn/`.

2. The link to download the *BoltBaitPack51.zip* file containing the installer is on the main page as shown in Figure 1-25. Click the link to download the zip file.

Figure 1-25. *The BoltBaitPack51.zip file is downloaded from the link indicated*

   3.   After it downloads, the zip file should be found in
the Downloads folder (Figure 1-26).

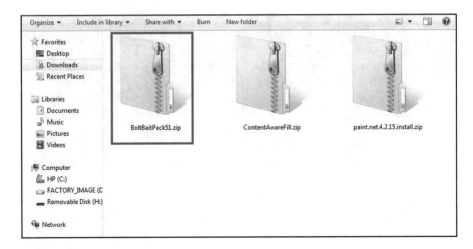

Figure 1-26. *The BoltBaitPack51.zip file in the Downloads folder*

4. Double-click the zip file; the *BoltBaitPack51.exe* file will be displayed (if a window indicating possible malware is displayed, you can simply continue without concern).

5. Double-click the .exe file; if the Windows Account dialog opens asking for permission to make changes to your system, click *Yes* to proceed.

6. The installation dialog window (Figure 1-27) is displayed; click the button agreeing to the license terms, then click the *Install everything* button.

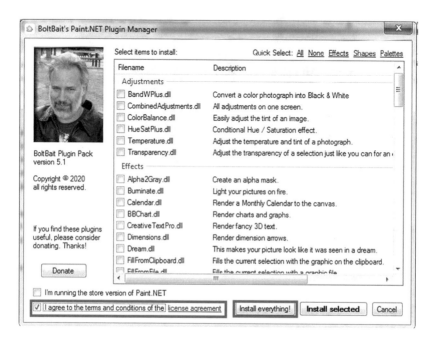

Figure 1-27. *Agree to the terms and conditions (read first), then click Install everything*

The plugins will now be installed. The plugins are indicated by a small puzzle piece icon as shown in Figure 1-28.

Figure 1-28. *Plugins are indicated by a puzzle piece–shaped icon*

Chapter Conclusion

This chapter covered a lot of territory, but by now you probably have a good sense of what this program can do.

Here's a recap of what was covered:

- System Requirements

- Acquiring and Installing Paint.NET

- The Main Window

- Menus

- The Settings Dialog

- The Color Scheme

- Supported File Formats

- Installing BoltBait's Plugin Pack

In Chapter 2, we'll learn all about using layers in Paint.NET and why they are important to image editing.

CHAPTER 2

Layers

Layers make working with digital images much easier. They allow you to correct mistakes or make revisions in your work without discarding the entire project and starting over. Changing the layer's Blend Mode can alter the way it interacts with the underlying layer, offering a variety of creative possibilities.

The topics covered in this chapter are

- Why Layers Are Important and How They Work

- Layer Blend Modes

- The Layers Menu

- The Layers Window

- Chapter Conclusion

Why Layers Are Important and How They Work

Layers can be thought of as clear transparencies—each one contains one or more graphical elements and is stacked one on top of another.

The concept illustration shown in Figure 2-1 demonstrates how the separate layers combine to form the composite image.

© Phillip Whitt 2022
P. Whitt, *Practical Paint.NET*, https://doi.org/10.1007/978-1-4842-7283-1_2

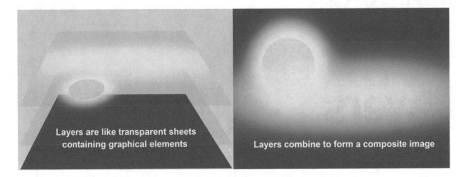

Figure 2-1. *Layers can be thought of as transparencies with graphical elements that combine to form the composite image*

The Importance of Layers

If you're new to image editing, the concept of layers might seem a bit intimidating (after all, traditional drawing or painting is typically done on a single sheet or canvas).

As you become more acquainted with Paint.NET, the importance of layers will become more apparent—they offer so much flexibility in terms of revising your work without having to start over from scratch. Layers also offer many creative possibilities.

Note   One important point I should make early on is that it's beneficial to name each new layer you create. Each time a new layer is created, Paint.NET assigns it a generic name (Layer 2, Layer 3, etc.). When a project is comprised of many layers, locating a specific one is much easier when they are named—this will be covered in more detail later in this chapter.

A Look at How Layers Work

Having a good working knowledge of layers will help you get the most out of using them. We'll now take a look at the basic aspects of working with layers and how they function.

Pixels and Transparency

When a new image (file) is created in Paint.NET, a white Background layer is generated by default. Each subsequent new layer created is transparent until pixels are added. Because transparent pixels can't be displayed, transparent areas of the layer are represented by a checkerboard pattern, as seen in Figure 2-2.

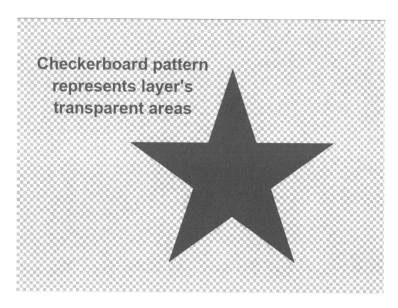

Figure 2-2. *Transparent areas of the layer are represented by a checkerboard pattern*

Layer Opacity

A layer's opacity can be adjusted from completely opaque to completely transparent. In most image editing programs, layer opacity is measured in percentage values ranging from 0% to 100%. In Paint.NET, layer opacity is measured in alpha values ranging from 0 (completely transparent) to 255 (completely opaque).

In Figure 2-3, the opacity is set to 135 using the slider in the Layer Properties dialog, making the layer partially transparent.

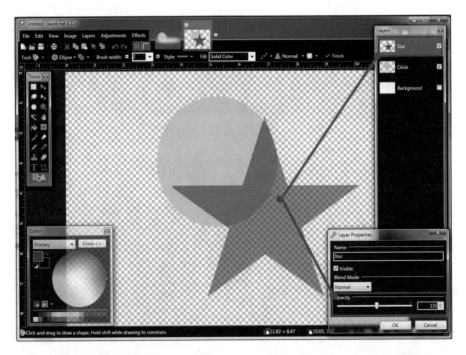

Figure 2-3. *The layer's opacity is adjusted using the slider in the Layer Properties dialog*

Note   An easy way to launch the Layer Properties dialog is to double-click the layer preview thumbnail in the Layers Window—this will be covered in more detail later in this chapter.

Layer Order

The layers can be reordered in the stack as needed. As shown in Figure 2-4, the layer containing the green circle is now positioned at the top of the stack. It's now above the layer containing the star, which now makes it visually appear at the forefront.

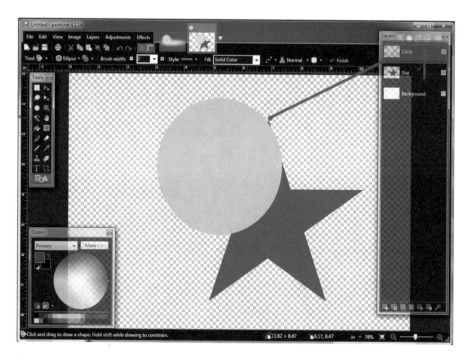

Figure 2-4. *Layers can be reordered in the layer stack as needed*

Layers can be reordered in the stack either by clicking and dragging the layer preview thumbnail up or down or by using the Up/Down buttons in the Layers Window, which will be covered in more detail later in this chapter.

Making a Layer Active

Clicking a layer thumbnail preview makes the corresponding layer *active*, meaning any editing or modification is confined to that layer only—the other layers are unaffected.

An active layer is indicated by the highlighted layer preview thumbnail. As we can see in Figure 2-5, using the Eraser on the active layer removes the pixels, but does not affect the rest of the image.

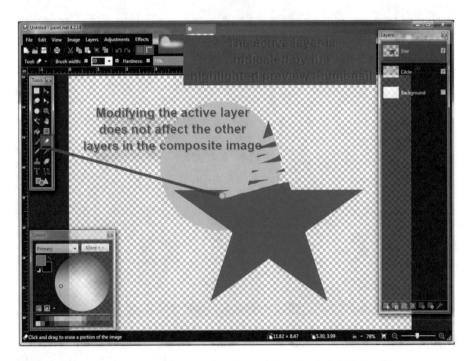

Figure 2-5. *The active layer is indicated by the highlighted thumbnail preview; any modifications only affect the active layer*

Layer Visibility

Layer visibility is toggled on and off by clicking the checkbox on the right side of the layer's preview thumbnail. As shown in Figure 2-6, when the box is unchecked, the layer containing the star is invisible. When the box is rechecked, the layer is now visible.

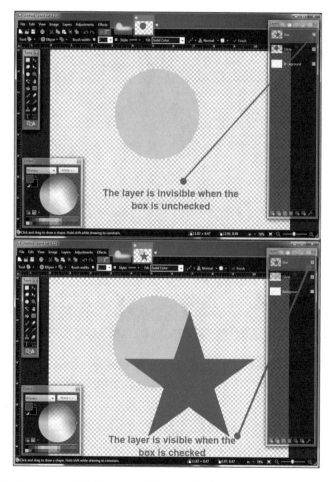

Figure 2-6. *Layer visibility can be toggled on and off by clicking the checkbox*

45

Repositioning Layers

The active layer can be repositioned by using the Move Selected Pixels
Tool or by using the arrow keys on the keyboard. When the pixels in a layer
are moved, the layer boundary temporarily moves and is indicated by an
active selection, and the vertical and horizontal rulers are highlighted
(Figure 2-7).

Figure 2-7. *The layer boundary is indicated by an active selection
that appears after the pixels in the layer are repositioned*

By deactivating the selection (Ctrl+D), the layer boundary returns to
its original position, even though the pixels on the layer are now in a new
position.

Layers can also be flipped (either vertically or horizontally), 180°, rotated, and zoomed in or out from the Layers Menu (Figure 2-8). The Layers Menu will be covered in more detail later in this chapter.

Figure 2-8. *The Layers Menu*

The Rotate/Zoom dialog shown in Figure 2-9 allows you to rotate, roll, pan, and zoom the pixels in or out (enlarge or reduce the size of the graphic in the layer).

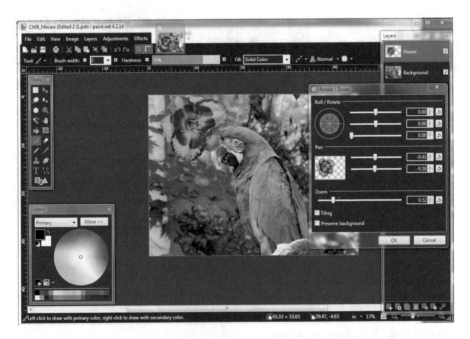

Figure 2-9. *The Rotate/Zoom dialog allows you to rotate, roll, pan, and enlarge or reduce the graphic in the active layer*

Layer Blend Modes

Blend Mode-i affect the way pixels of one layer interact with pixels of another. Paint.NET offers 14 blend modes (including the default Normal).

Figure 2-10 shows how the layer of the flower on the top layer interacts with the layer below in each blend mode.

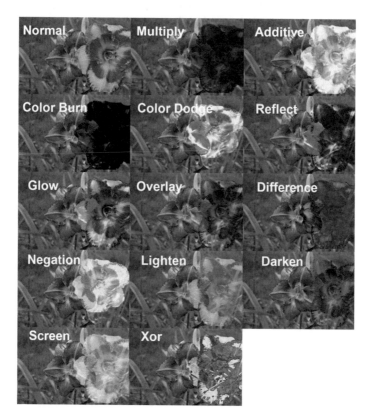

Figure 2-10. *An example of how each blend mode of the top layer interacts with the layer below*

The blend mode descriptions are as follows:

- **Normal**—The default blend mode; each pixel interacts with the layers in the composite based on alpha values. Fully opaque areas completely obscure the pixels in the layers below. Partially opaque areas of the layer obscure the underlying pixels accordingly.

- **Multiply**—The RGB component intensity value of each pixel of the top layer is multiplied with that of the pixels in the underlying layer. The result is a darker composite image. White pixels essentially become transparent.

- **Additive**—This blend mode adds the pixel intensity values of one layer with those from the composition. The pixels become brighter, while black pixels become transparent.

- **Color Burn**—This blend mode makes dark pixels darker; lighter pixels are blended with light colored pixels to remain bright.

- **Color Dodge**—This blend mode works in the opposite manner than Color Burn does. Light pixels retain their brightness, while darker pixels are blended with other dark pixels to remain dark.

- **Reflect**—This blend mode is useful for adding "shiny" areas of light; black pixels in the blend layer are rendered as though transparent.

- **Glow**—This blend mode essentially brightens the composite image by the amount of brightness in the blend layer; black pixels in the blend layer are rendered as though transparent.

- **Overlay**—This blend mode adds contrast to the composite image by increasing the intensity of light and dark colors; light colors are lightened more (as the Screen blend mode acts), and dark colors are darkened more (as the Multiply blend mode acts).

- **Difference**—This blend mode subtracts the layer's pixel intensity of the composite's pixel intensity resulting in darker colors. Blending with black produces no change; blending with white inverts the picture.

- **Negation**—This blend mode produces the opposite effect of the difference blend mode, creating lighter colors.

- **Lighten**—This blend mode uses the lightest pixel of either the blend layer or the composite.

- **Darken**—This blend mode uses the darkest pixel of either the blend layer or the composite.

- **Screen**—This blend mode works in the opposite manner as Multiply; it's used to make pixels in the composite brighter, while black pixels are rendered transparent.

- **Xor**—An abbreviation of "exclusive OR," this blend mode is used mainly for image analysis. Pixels in the blend layer which exactly match the composition will be rendered black. Where differences exist, colors are shown. This blend mode can also be used to create interesting "surreal" color effects, as we'll see later in this book.

Note   My intention was to simplify the blend mode descriptions in this section as much as possible. They are adapted from the descriptions in the Layer Blend Modes section in the Paint.NET documentation (which are a bit more technical) found here: `www.getpaint.net/doc/latest/BlendModes.html`.

The Layers Menu

All of the major layer functions can be carried out from the Layers Menu. As was explained in Chapter 1, the Layers Menu is accessed from the Menu Bar (Figure 2-11).

Figure 2-11. *The Layers Menu is accessed from the Menu Bar*

Here's a brief description of each function, with the corresponding keyboard shortcut (not all functions have keyboard shortcuts):

- **Add New Layer** (Ctrl+Shift+N)—Creates a new layer above the currently active layer.

- **Delete Layer** (Ctrl+Shift+Del)—Removes the currently active layer.

- **Duplicate Layer** (Ctrl+Shift+D)—Creates a copy of the currently active layer.

- **Merge Layer Down** (Ctrl+Shift+M)—Merges the currently active layer to the layer just below, combining the two into a single layer.

- **Import From File**—Imports an image as a layer; if the dimensions of the imported image are larger than the composite, the layer boundary expands accordingly. If the image is a layered Paint.NET file, all of the layers are imported separately.

- **Flip Horizontal**—Flips (reverses) the active layer horizontally.

- **Flip Vertical**—Flips the active layer vertically.

- **Rotate 180°**—Rotates the active layer in a clockwise direction 180°.

- **Rotate/Zoom**—Launches a dialog that allows you to roll, rotate, pan (move back and forth or up and down), or enlarge or reduce the graphical elements in an active layer.

- **Go to Top Layer**—Moves to the top layer, making it active; the function is grayed out if the top layer is already active.

- **Go to Layer Below**—Moves from the currently active layer to the one just below, making it the active layer; the function is grayed out if the active layer is at the bottom of the stack.

- **Go to Bottom Layer** (Ctrl+Alt+PgDn)—Moves the bottom layer, making it active; the icon is grayed out and the function unavailable if the bottom layer is already active.

- **Move Layer to Top**—Moves the currently active layer to the top of the layer stack; the icon is grayed out and the function unavailable if the top layer is active.

- **Move Layer Up**—Moves the currently active layer up one level in the layer stack; the icon is grayed out and the function unavailable if the top layer is active.

- **Move Layer Down**—Moves the currently active layer down one level in the layer stack; the icon is grayed out and the function unavailable when the top layer is active.

- **Move Layer to Bottom**—Moves the currently active layer to the bottom of the layer stack; the icon is grayed out and the function unavailable when the bottom layer is active.

- **Layer Properties**—Opens the Layer Properties dialog. This dialog allows you to

  - Name the layer

  - Activate/deactivate layer visibility

  - Change the blend mode

  - Adjust the layer opacity

The Layer Properties dialog is shown in Figure 2-12.

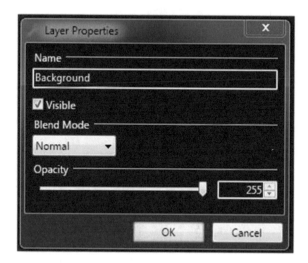

Figure 2-12. *The Layer Properties dialog*

The Layers Window

The Layers Window (Figure 2-13) displays the layer preview thumbnail images and offers some of the same functions as those in the Layers Menu.

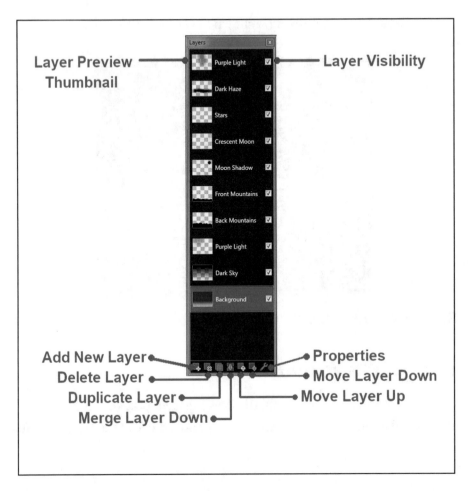

Figure 2-13. *The Layers Window*

The functions available in the Layers Window are

- Layer preview thumbnail

- Layer visibility

- Add new layer

- Delete layer

- Duplicate layer

- Merge layer

- Properties

- Move layer down

- Move layer up

Chapter Conclusion

By now, I'm sure the value of layers is obvious. Here's a brief recap of what was covered:

- Why Layers Are Important and How They Work

- Pixels and Transparency

- How Layers Work

- Layer Blend Modes

- The Layers Menu

- The Layers Window

Now that you have a good working understanding of layers, let's move on to Chapter 3 and learn about the tools used in Paint.NET.

CHAPTER 3

An Overview of the Paint.NET Tools

Paint.NET offers a modest yet capable set of tools to help you with your image editing and creation projects. In this chapter, we'll take a look at the tools available to you in Paint.NET and how they work.

The topics covered in this chapter are

- Accessing the Tools
- The Selection Tools
- The Move Tools
- The View Tools
- The Fill Tools
- The Drawing Tools
- The Photo Tools
- The Text and Shape Tools
- Chapter Conclusion

Accessing the Tools

Tools can be accessed from either the Tools Window or the Tools Menu. As was mentioned in Chapter 1, the Tools, History, Layers, and Colors Windows can be toggled off when needed. These windows can sometimes obstruct the view of your work on the canvas (particularly if you are using a small monitor), and toggling them off can be an advantage for increased screen real estate.

The Tools Menu provides access to the tools when you need them if keeping the Tools Window is preferred. Figure 3-1 shows both the Tools Menu and Tools Window.

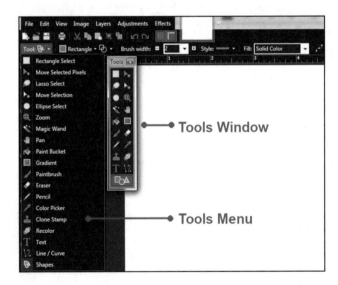

Figure 3-1. *Paint.NET's tools can be accessed from either the Tools Window or the Tools Menu*

The Selection Tools

The Selection Tools are used to isolate a specific area (or multiple areas) of an image. The selected area can be edited without affecting the areas outside of the selection.

The *Rectangle Select, Lasso Select,* and *Ellipse Select Tools* work by clicking and dragging around an area or areas of the image. The *Magic Wand* makes selections by detecting areas of similar color.

Table 3-1 provides a look at the Paint.NET Selection Tool icons, along with the keyboard shortcuts and a brief description of how they work.

Table 3-1. *The Selection Tools Available in Paint.NET*

Tool	Keyboard Shortcut	Description
Rectangle Select	S	Makes rectangular shaped selections. Makes square selections when the Shift key is held.
Lasso Select	S,S	Makes freehand selections around irregularly shaped objects.
Ellipse Select	S,S,S	Makes elliptical shaped selections. Makes circular selections when the Shift key is held.
Magic Wand	S,S,S,S	Selects areas of similar color.

Selection Modes

Paint.NET utilizes five types of *Selection Modes*, allowing the user to modify an active selection:

- **Replace**—This is the default mode; when a new selection is made, it replaces the previous one.

- **Add (Union)**—This mode allows you to add to an existing selection or make multiple selections.

- **Subtract**—This mode allows you to subtract from an existing selection.

- **Intersect**—In this mode, only overlapping selection areas are kept. The areas outside of the new selection are removed.

- **Invert (Xor)**—This mode works in a similar manner to the Add mode; the main difference is that overlapping areas become deselected, while the outside areas remain selected.

Figure 3-2 provides a basic visual aid for each selection mode.

Figure 3-2. *The five Selection Modes in Paint.NET*

Flood Mode and Tolerance (Magic Wand)

The Flood Mode offers two settings: *Contiguous* and *Global* (Figure 3-3). The Contiguous setting selects neighboring pixels in a color range, while the Global setting selects all of the pixels within a color range (regardless if they are connected or not). The Tolerance setting increases or decreases the color range of the selected pixels.

Figure 3-3. *The Flood Mode and Tolerance settings are used for the Magic Wand*

Selection Quality

There are two settings for selection quality: *Pixelated* and *Antialiased*. The Pixelated setting results in a jagged edge, while the Antialiased setting results in a smoother selection edge. The difference between these two selection qualities is shown in Figure 3-4.

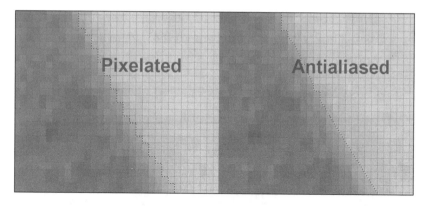

Figure 3-4. *The Pixelated and Antialiased quality settings comparison*

Selection Modification Plugins

BoltBait's Plugin Pack (that was mentioned in Chapter 1) includes plugins for five different settings to modify selections:

- **Bevel Selection**—Applies a bevel effect, giving the selected area a somewhat 3D look; a dialog box is launched that allows the user to adjust the setting parameters.

- **Blur Selection Edge**—Similar to antialias, smooths the selection edge by blurring slightly.

- **Feather Selection**—Applies a soft edge to the selection; a dialog box is launched that allows the user to adjust the feather setting from one to ten.

- **Inner Shadow**—Applies a shadow inside the selection; a dialog box is launched that allows the user to adjust the shadow setting parameters.

- **Outline Selection**—Applies an outline to a selection; a dialog box is launched that allows the user to adjust the outline setting parameters.

The BoltBait plugins for modifying selections are shown in Figure 3-5.

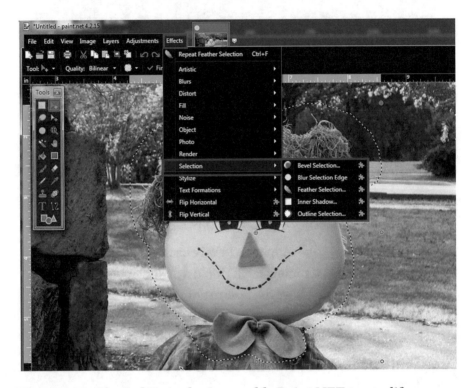

Figure 3-5. *The BoltBait plugins enable Paint.NET to modify selections*

Note   The Paint.NET plugins web page can be found here: www. getpaint.net/doc/latest/InstallPlugins.html—the plugin forum web page can be found here: https://forums. getpaint.net/forum/7-plugins-publishing-only/

The Move Tools

There are two tools in this category: the *Move Selected Pixels Tool* and the *Move Selection Tool.* Table 3-2 provides a quick look at them.

Table 3-2. *The Move Tools Available in Paint.NET*

Tool	Keyboard Shortcut	Description
Move Selected Pixels	M	Moves the pixels contained within a selection; if no selection is made, all the pixels in the layer are moved.
Move Selection	M,M	Moves only the outline of a selection.

Figure 3-6 provides a visual example of each tool in use and how they differ.

Figure 3-6. *The Move Selected Pixels and Move Selection tool comparison*

When the Move Selected Pixels Tool is active, hold the Control (Ctrl) key to create a copy of the selected area (Figure 3-7).

***Figure 3-7.** Holding the Control (Ctrl) key creates a copy of the selected pixels when moved*

Note   When either of the Move tools is active and the mouse cursor is hovered over the selection, it becomes a four-way arrow, indicating the selection can then be moved.

Selection Control Nubs

When either move tool is active, there are *Control Nubs* (Figure 3-8) that appear as small circles along the selection. The Control Nubs allow the user to alter the shape or size of the selection when a Control Nub is clicked and dragged; holding the Shift key maintains the selection proportions when resizing.

Figure 3-8. *The Control Nubs are used to alter the shape or size of the selection*

Note   When hovering the cursor over a Control Nub, it becomes a hand-shaped icon indicating it can then be clicked and dragged to alter the selection.

Rotating Selections

When either move tool is active, the selection can be freely rotated in either a clockwise or counter-clockwise direction (Figure 3-9).

Figure 3-9. *The selection can be freely rotated either clockwise or counter-clockwise*

Note   When hovering the cursor just outside the selection and it becomes a double-headed curved arrow, the selection can then be rotated.

Resampling Modes

There are three resampling modes available in the Tool Bar when resizing selected pixels: *Nearest Neighbor, Bilinear,* and *Bicubic.*

Bilinear is the default setting (Figure 3-10). Nearest Neighbor is the lowest quality setting and can produce pixelated results. Bicubic is the highest quality setting, but is more computer resource demanding.

Figure 3-10.   *The default Bilinear setting is the mid-quality resampling setting*

The View Tools

There are two tools in this category: the *Zoom Tool* and the *Pan Tool*.
Table 3-3 provides a quick look at them.

Table 3-3. *The Zoom and Pan Tools*

Tool	Keyboard Shortcut	Description
Zoom	Z	The Zoom Tool is used to enlarge or reduce the image view. When the Zoom Tool is active, clicking the left mouse button enlarges the view; right-clicking reduces the view.
		Clicking and dragging around an area enlarges the view of that area.
		The image view can be enlarged or reduced by holding the Control (Ctrl) key and using the mouse scrolling wheel.
Pan	H	The Pan Tool is used to scroll through an image when it's larger than the editing window—this action can also be performed (without the Pan Tool being active) by holding the Spacebar while clicking and dragging the image.

Overscrolling

Overscrolling means scrolling the image past the edge of the editing window (Figure 3-11). This can be disabled by opening the Settings dialog and unchecking the overscroll setting.

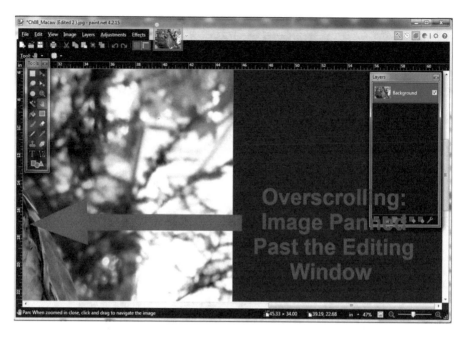

Figure 3-11. *An example of overscrolling*

Centering the Image

The image can be centered by pressing Ctrl+B twice; the first entry of these keys zooms the image to the window, and the second displays the image at the previous zoom level (Figure 3-12). This can also be done by using View ➤ Zoom to Window twice.

Figure 3-12. *Centering the image using the Ctrl+B keys*

The Fill Tools

There are two tools in this category: the *Paint Bucket* and the *Gradient*. Table 3-4 provides a quick look at them.

Table 3-4. *The Paint Bucket and Gradient Tools*

Tool		Keyboard Shortcut	Description
	Paint Bucket	F	The Paint Bucket Tool is used to fill areas of a similar color with another color or hue; it can also fill areas with one of numerous available patterns from the Fill Style menu.
	Gradient	G	The Gradient Tool fills an area with a gradual blending from one color to another.
			There are seven types and multiple formats available.

The Paint Bucket Tool

This tool is used to fill an area of one color with another or with a pattern. A basic example of that operation is shown in Figure 3-13.

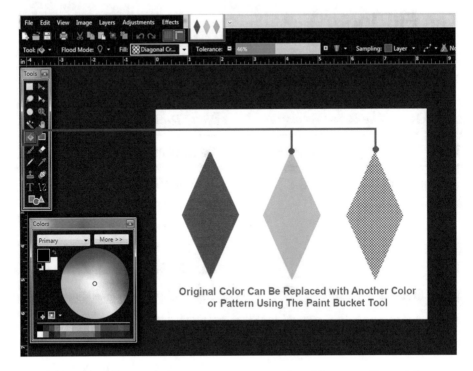

Figure 3-13. *The Paint Bucket Tool is used to fill one color with another color or pattern*

By default, the Paint Bucket Tool fills an area with a solid color. By clicking the *Fill Type* menu on the Tool Bar, an area can be filled with a pattern selected from the sub-menu (Figure 3-14). The pattern color will be the same as the Primary Color setting in the Colors Window.

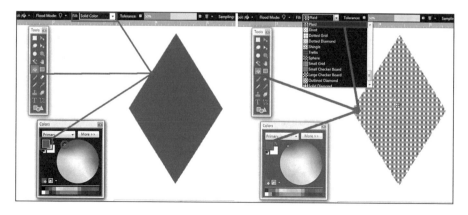

Figure 3-14. *By default, the Paint Bucket Tool fills with a solid color, but a pattern can be selected from the Fill Type menu on the Tool Bar*

Flood Mode and Tolerance (Paint Bucket Tool)

The Paint Bucket Tool's *Flood Mode* operates in a similar manner as it does for the Magic Wand (which was covered earlier in this chapter). It detects pixels within a certain color range.

Instead of selecting pixels (as the Magic Wand does), it fills an area of a color range with either another color or pattern.

The *Contiguous* setting fills neighboring pixels within a specific color range, while the *Global* setting fills all of the pixels within a specific color range (regardless if they are connected or not). The *Tolerance* setting increases or decreases the color range of the selected pixels. Figure 3-15 shows the original image, and the tolerance levels set at 30%, 40%, and 50%.

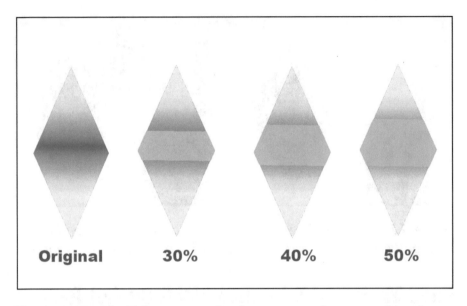

Figure 3-15. *The Tolerance setting increases or decreases the color range of pixels filled*

Changing an Active Fill Color

As Figure 3-16 illustrates, the fill color can be changed at will while the fill is still active, but can no longer be done once the fill operation is completed.

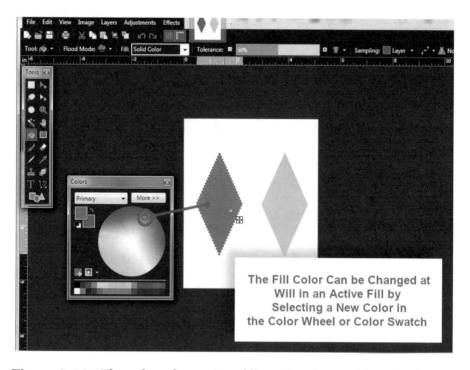

Figure 3-16. *The color of an active fill can be changed by selecting a new color in the color wheel or color swatch*

Dragging the Click Point

By clicking and dragging the *Control Nub* (a white square with four arrows pointing outward), the click point is interpenetrated, thus changing the fill. In Figure 3-17, clicking and dragging the Control Nub to the left expands the red color fill to include the diamond shape.

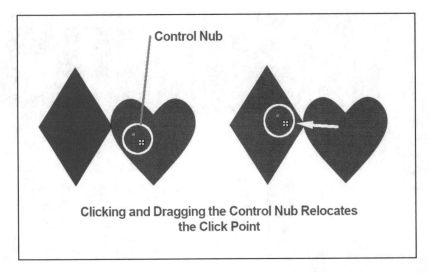

Figure 3-17. *Clicking and dragging the Control Nub relocates the click point*

The Gradient Tool

The Gradient Tool is used to make a transition from one color to another. Holding the left mouse button draws a gradient with the Primary Color transitioning to the Secondary Color. Holding the right mouse button reverses the order, drawing a gradient with the Secondary Color transitioning to the Primary Color (Figure 3-18).

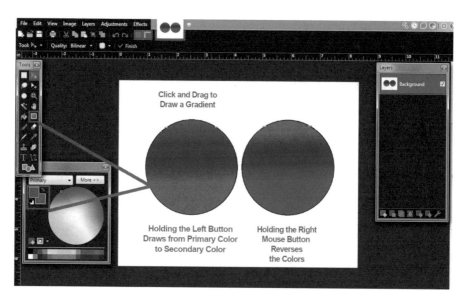

Figure 3-18. *Holding the left mouse button draws the gradient with the Primary Color transitioning to the Secondary Color; holding the right mouse button reverses the colors*

Gradient Types

There are seven types available, shown in Figure 3-19.

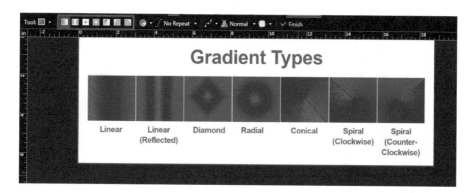

Figure 3-19. *There are seven gradient types available*

The gradient types are

- Linear

- Linear(Reflected)

- Diamond

- Radial

- Conical

- Spiral (Clockwise)

- Spiral (Counter-Clockwise)

Color Mode/Transparency

Gradients can be drawn using one of two modes: the *Color Mode* or the
Transparency Mode. The Color Mode uses the Primary and Secondary
Colors, while the Transparency Mode transitions from white to transparent
(Figure 3-20).

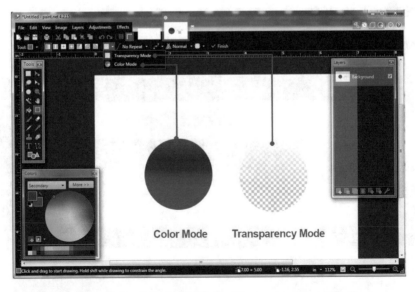

Figure 3-20. *The Color Mode and the Transparency Mode*

The Repeat Modes

The *Repeat Modes* affect how the gradient behaves beyond edges of the shape. The three modes are *No Repeat, Repeat Wrapped,* and *Repeat Reflected* (Figure 3-21).

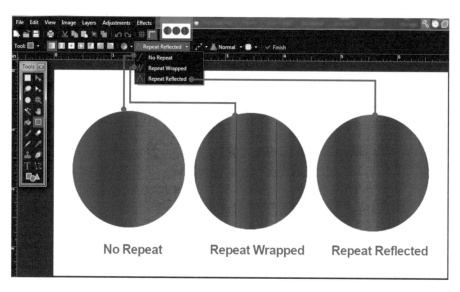

Figure 3-21. *The Gradient Repeat Modes*

Antialiasing Enabled/Disabled

When enabled, this setting smooths hard edges; when disabled, hard edges have a more jagged appearance.

Blend Modes

The Blend Mode of a gradient can be changed, altering the way it interacts with the image. Figure 3-22 shows an example of a gradient set to the Normal Blend Mode and the Difference Blend Mode.

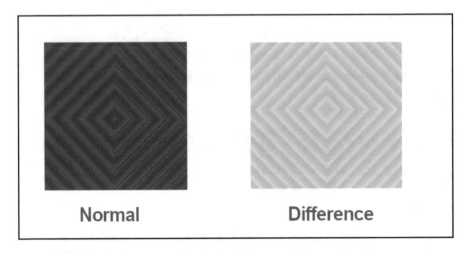

Figure 3-22. *The Normal and Difference Blend Modes*

The Drawing Tools

The three drawing tools (the *Paintbrush, Eraser,* and *Pencil Tools*) emulate their real-world counterparts. The Paintbrush and Pencil Tools apply color to an image, while the Eraser Tool removes pixels.

Table 3-5 provides a quick look at these tools.

Table 3-5. *The Drawing Tools*

Tool	Keyboard Shortcut	Description
Paintbrush	B	The Paintbrush Tool is used to apply color in much the same way a real-world paintbrush works. It also applies patterns. The brush width, hardness, blend mode, and selection quality can be adjusted or changed.
Eraser	E	The Eraser Tool removes pixels—in a single-layer image, the transparent areas are exposed, or the pixels of the underlying layer are shown. The brush width, hardness, and selection quality can be adjusted.
Pencil	P	The Pencil Tool applies color in a hard, 1 pixel wide stroke. The blend mode can be changed.

The Paintbrush Tool

The Paintbrush Tool is used to apply color in a similar way a real-world paintbrush does. By default, holding the left mouse button while dragging applies the Primary Color set in the Colors Window. Holding the right mouse button applies the secondary color (Figure 3-23).

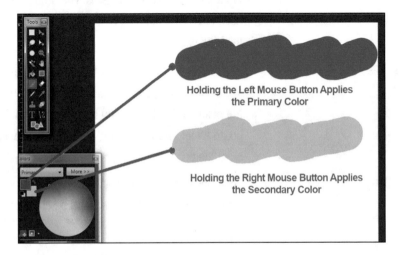

Figure 3-23. *Holding the left mouse button applies the Primary Color, while holding the right mouse button applies the secondary color*

By adjusting the *Opacity-Alpha* setting in the Colors Window (click the *More* button to expose this setting), holding the left mouse button while painting applies the alpha setting of the Primary Color, resulting in partial transparency.

When the Opacity-Alpha setting is applied to the secondary color, holding the right mouse button while painting applies partially transparent strokes (Figure 3-24).

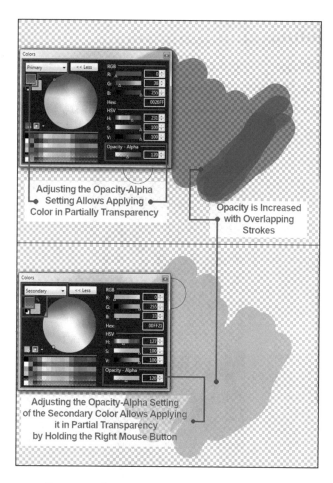

Figure 3-24. Adjusting the Opacity-Alpha setting allows partially transparent paint strokes

The amount of transparency can range from complete transparency (zero coverage) to no transparency (total coverage), depending on the setting.

Brush Width

The brush width ranges from 1 pixel up to 2000 pixels wide. It is set from the *Brush width* menu on the Tool Bar (Figure 3-25). The brush width can also be changed using the bracket keys ([ ]). The left key decreases the brush width, while the right key increases the brush width.

Figure 3-25. *The brush width ranges from 1 pixel to 2000 pixels*

Brush Hardness

The brush hardness can be set from 0% hardness (with a soft edge) to 100% hardness (with a hard edge) from the *Hardness slider* on the Tool Bar. Figure 3-26 shows examples of the brush strokes at 0% hardness, 50% hardness, and 100% hardness.

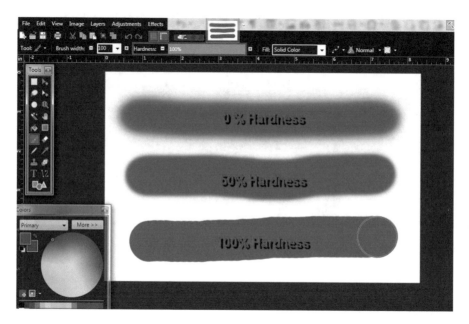

Figure 3-26. *The brush hardness can be set from 0% hardness to 100% hardness*

Fill Style

The Paintbrush Tool applies a solid color by default, but by using the *Fill Menu*, there are numerous styles of patterns to choose from. The example in Figure 3-27 shows the *Horizontal Brick* pattern with the primary and secondary colors.

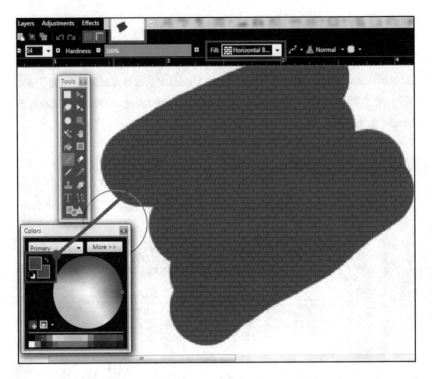

Figure 3-27. *This example shows the Horizontal Brick pattern using the primary and secondary colors*

Blend Modes

Like the Paint Bucket and Gradient Tools, the Paintbrush Tool's blend mode can be changed from the menu on the Tool Bar (Figure 3-28).

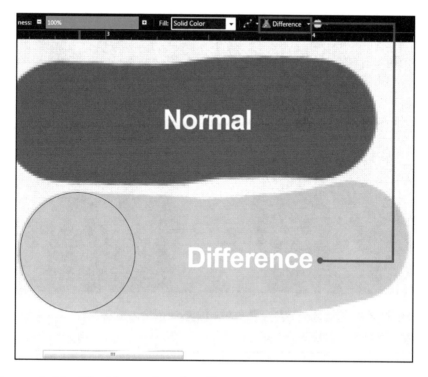

Figure 3-28. *The Normal and Difference Blend Modes*

Antialias Enabled/Disabled Setting

When Antialias is enabled, the brush edge is smoother than the edge created when it's disabled (which is more jagged) as shown in Figure 3-29.

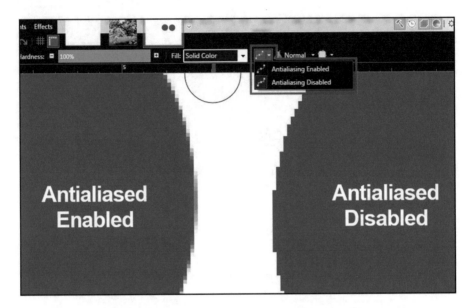

Figure 3-29. *The Antialias Enabled setting creates a smoother edge*

The Eraser Tool

The Eraser Tool is used to remove pixels from the image (or active layer). As shown in Figure 3-30, using the Eraser Tool removes the pixels of a single-layered image, showing areas of transparency. When pixels are removed on a layer in a multi-layered image, the pixels of the underlying layer are revealed.

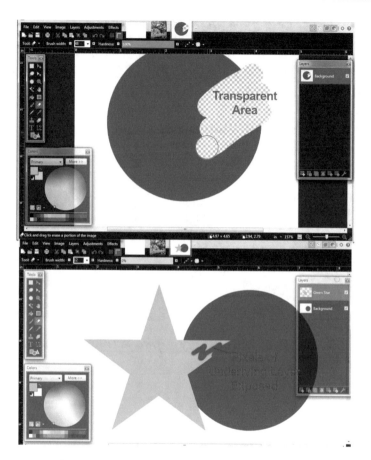

Figure 3-30. *The Eraser Tool removes pixels, revealing a transparent area in a single-layered image, or the pixels in the underlying layer of a multi-layered image*

Like the Paintbrush Tool, the brush width ranges from 1 pixel to 2000 pixels, and the brush hardness ranges from 0% hardness (soft) to 100% hardness. Antialiasing can also be enabled or disabled.

By adjusting the Opacity-Alpha setting of the Primary Color in the Colors Window, pixels can be removed leaving partial opacity (Figure 3-31). The amount of opacity can range from 0% to 100%, depending on the setting.

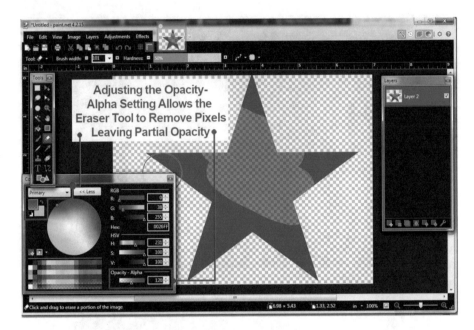

Figure 3-31. *Adjusting the Opacity-Alpha Setting allows partially transparent color to be applied*

The Pencil Tool

The Pencil Tool draws a 1 pixel wide stroke. Unlike the Paintbrush Tool, there are no options to adjust the width or hardness. However, the blend mode can be changed, and the Opacity-Alpha setting can be adjusted in the Colors Window to draw a partially transparent stroke. Figure 3-32 shows an example of a stroke drawn in the Normal Blend Mode, the Difference Blend Mode, and with partial transparency.

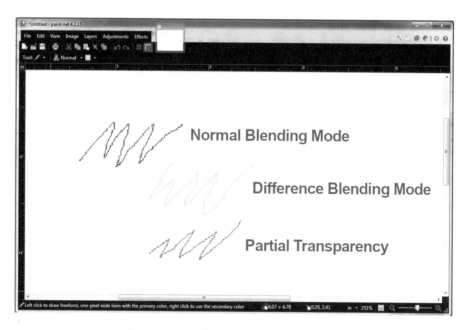

Figure 3-32. *The Pencil Tool draws a hard, 1 pixel wide stroke*

The Photo Tools

The three photo tools (the *Color Picker, Clone Stamp,* and *Recolor Tools*) are used primarily for enhancing and retouching digital photographs.

Table 3-6 provides a quick look at these tools.

Table 3-6. *The Photo Tools*

Tool	Keyboard Shortcut	Description
Color Picker	K	The Color Picker Tool is used to sample a color from the active layer and to set it as the primary or secondary color.
Clone Stamp	L	The Clone Stamp Tool is used to copy pixels from one area and paste onto another (on one layer or between layers). This tool is extremely useful for photo retouching.
Recolor	R	The Recolor Tool replaces one color with another.

The Color Picker

The Color Picker is used to sample colors in the active layer or image and sets either the primary or secondary color slot with the sampled color, as shown in Figure 3-33.

Figure 3-33. *The Color Picker samples a color from the active layer*

Note   To set the secondary color, click the *Swap Colors* (a double-headed curved arrow) command, or press the keyboard shortcut X.

Sampling Modes

The Color Picker has two *sampling modes*: Image and Layer (Figure 3-34). In the Image mode, pixels are sampled from the composite image (as if the image were flattened into a single-layered image). In the Layer mode, the pixels are sampled from the active layer.

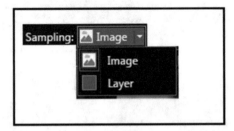

Figure 3-34. *The two sampling modes are Image and Layer*

Sampling Sizes

There are six sampling sizes that the Color Picker uses: 1 pixel, 3x3, 5x5, 11x11, 31x31, and 51x51 (Figure 3-35). The size determines the area that will be used when setting the color slot.

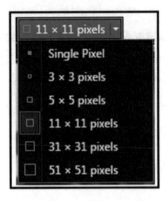

Figure 3-35. *The Sampling Sizes menu*

When a range of colors are sampled (by a setting of more than 1 pixel), an average is calculated, and the color slot is set to a single hue.

After Click

The Color Picker provides these three options (Figure 3-36) after the tool is used:

- **Do not switch tool**—This leaves the Color Picker as the active tool after a color has been sampled.

- **Switch to previous tool**—Once a color has been sampled, it reverts to the last tool that was used.

- **Switch to Pencil tool**—Once a color has been sampled, the Pencil Tool becomes active.

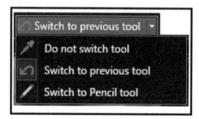

Figure 3-36. *The After Click options*

The Clone Stamp Tool

This tool is indispensable in photo retouching and restoration work. It essentially samples pixels from one area of the layer or image and then "pastes" them over another. Figure 3-37 shows an example of power lines being digitally removed from the image (which will be in a tutorial later in this book).

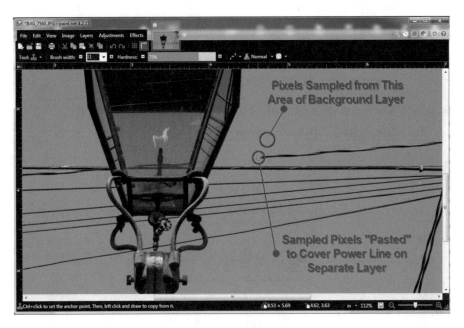

Figure 3-37. *The Clone Stamp Tool being used to digitally remove power lines from the image*

Like the Paintbrush Tool, the brush width ranges from 1 pixel to 2000 pixels, and the brush hardness ranges from 0% hardness (soft) to 100% hardness. Antialiasing can also be enabled or disabled.

Blend Modes are also available to the Clone Stamp Tool. Figure 3-38 shows an example of the Clone Stamp Tool set to the Difference Blend Mode; an effect similar to a photographic negative is achieved.

Figure 3-38. *The Clone Stamp Tool set to the Difference Blend Mode*

The Recolor Tool

This tool provides a quick and easy means of replacing areas of one color with another (using the Primary Color in the Colors Window). Figure 3-39 shows an example of the red car interior being replaced with blue.

Figure 3-39. *The Recolor Tool replaces one color with another*

Like the Paintbrush Tool, the brush width ranges from 1 pixel to 2000 pixels, and the brush hardness ranges from 0% hardness (soft) to 100% hardness. Antialiasing can also be enabled or disabled.

Tolerance

This setting adjusts the range (sensitivity) of the color replaced. The higher the tolerance setting, the wider range of pixels will be affected (Figure 3-40).

Figure 3-40. *A comparison of the Recolor Tool's tolerance set 20% and 60%*

Tolerance Alpha Mode

The two alpha modes available are *Premultiplied* and *Straight*:

- **Premultiplied**—This Alpha Mode results in transparent pixels being equally affected, even if the RGB (color) channel values are different.

- **Straight**—The Straight Alpha Mode results in transparent pixels being affected equally only if the RGB (color) channel values are also equal.

Figure 3-41 shows the Tolerance Alpha Mode menu.

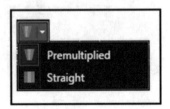

Figure 3-41. *The Tolerance Alpha Mode menu*

Sampling: Once/Sampling: Secondary Color

Here's a brief explanation of how the *Sampling: Once* and *Sampling: Secondary Color* modes work:

- **Sampling: Once**—Uses the color that you click at the start of a brush stroke. When the left mouse button is used, it recolors the color *first clicked* with the Primary Color. Using the right mouse button recolors the color *first clicked* with the Secondary Color.

- **Sampling: Secondary Color**—Uses the Secondary Color in the Colors Window. When the left mouse button is used, the Primary Color becomes the replacement color; pixels within the tolerance of the Secondary Color will be replaced. When the right mouse button is used, the roles of the colors are switched.

The Text and Shape Tools

This group of tools consists of the *Text Tool, Line/Curve Tool,* and the *Shapes Tool.* Table 3-7 provides a quick look at these tools.

Table 3-7. *The Text Tool, Line/Curve Tool, and Shapes Tool*

Tool	Keyboard Shortcut	Description
Text	T	The Text Tool is used to place text on the active layer.
Line/Curve	O	This tool is used to draw straight or curved lines.
Shapes	O,O	This tool contains a variety of preconfigured shapes that can be applied to an active layer.

The Text Tool

This tool is used to apply text (using the Primary Color) to an active layer (Figure 3-42).

Figure 3-42. *The Text Tool is used to add text to an active layer*

The Text Tool Options

When active, the Text Tool options are displayed on the Tool Bar, as shown in Figure 3-43.

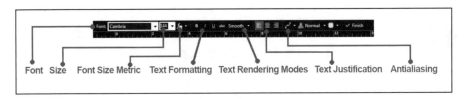

Figure 3-43. *The Text Tool options*

These options are

- **Font**—This menu allows you to select the font (typeface) that will be used in the text.

- **Size**—Selects the font size, 8 points being the smallest and 288 points being the largest.

- **Font Size Metric**—*Points* render the text to be scaled to the image DPI. *Fixed* displays the text in to match the Windows monitor resolution of 96 DPI.

- **Text Formatting**—Displays text in bold, italics, underline, strikeout, or all simultaneously.

- **Text Rendering Modes**—The three rendering modes are *Smooth, Sharp (Modern)*, and *Sharp (Classic)*.

- **Text Justification**—This is the direction that typed text will extend away from the initial cursor position: *Align Left, Center Align*, and *Align Right* (Figure 3-44).

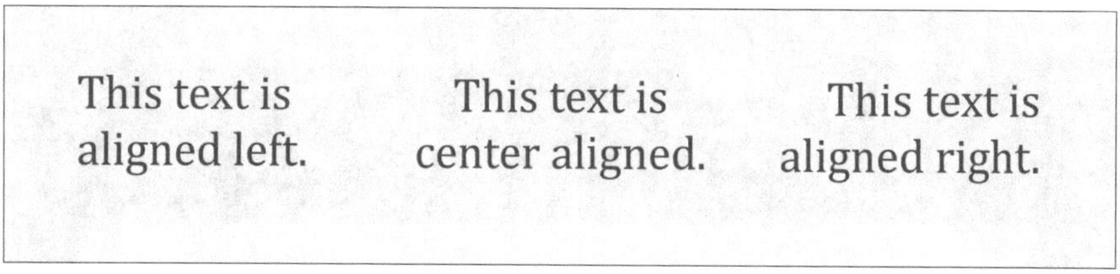

This text is aligned left.	This text is center aligned.	This text is aligned right.

Figure 3-44. *Examples of text aligned left, center, and right*

- **Antialiasing Enabled/Disabled**—Enabling this option smooths the edges of the text; disabling creates a more jagged edge.

The Line/Curve Tool

This tool is used to draw straight or curved lines. After a straight line has been drawn, it can be curved using the Control Nubs (Figure 3-45). Before the line or curve is committed to the canvas, it can be moved anywhere by dragging the Move icon. The line or curve can be rotated by hovering the cursor outside of the line or curve; when the cursor changes into a curved double-headed arrow, it can be rotated.

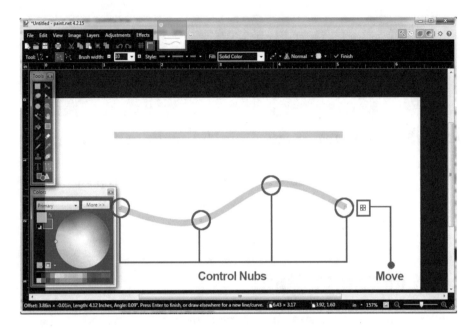

Figure 3-45. *The Control Nubs and the Move icon*

The Line/Curve Tool Options

When active, the Line/Curve Tool options are displayed on the Tool Bar, as shown in Figure 3-46.

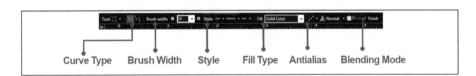

Figure 3-46. *The Line/Curve Tool options*

These options are

- **Curve Type**—This allows a choice of two settings: *Spline* and *Bezier*. The Spline setting places four Control Nubs along the line, which continues through the nubs. The Bezier setting places four Control Nubs along the line, but two of them (second and third) don't always stay in contact with the line (Figure 3-47).

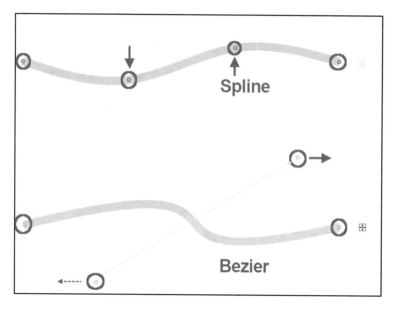

Figure 3-47. *The Spline and Bezier Curve Types*

- **Brush Width**—The line width can range from 1 pixel to 2000 pixels.

- *Style*—Offers a variety of styles that can be applied to the line: Flat, Arrow (left and right pointing), Filled Arrow (left and right pointing), Rounded, Solid, Dashes, Dotted, Dash-Dot, Dash-Dot-Dot (Figure 3-48).

Figure 3-48. *The Style options*

- **Fill Type**—Fills the line/curve with a solid color or a
  pattern.

- **Antialiasing Enabled/Disabled**—Enabling this option
  smooths the edges of the line/curve; disabling creates a
  more jagged edge.

- **Blend Mode**—Applies a blend mode to the line/curve.

The Shapes Tool

This tool offers a variety of predesigned shapes, ranging from basic
geometric shapes to vehicles (Figure 3-49). Shapes can be resized (either
proportionally or disproportionately) by using the Control Nubs and can
also be rotated before committing to the canvas.

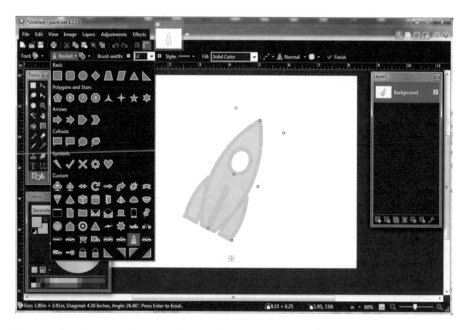

Figure 3-49. *The Shapes Tool offers a variety of predesigned shapes*

Using the *Shape/Draw Fill Mode*, a shape can be rendered with just an outline, a fill with no outline, or a fill with an outline (Figure 3-50).

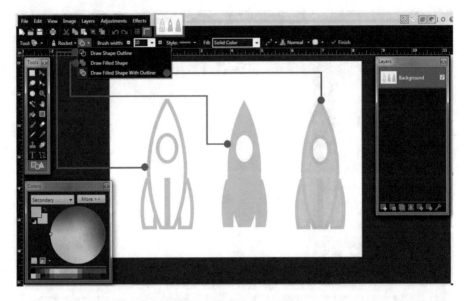

Figure 3-50. *The Shape/Draw Fill Mode renders an outline only, fill only, or both outline and fill*

Like the Line/Curve Tool, the Shapes Tool shares these options:

- **Brush Width**—The shape outline width can range from 1 pixel to 2000 pixels.

- **Style**—This option allows the shape outline to be comprised of one of these styles: Solid, Dashes, Dotted, Dash-Dot, Dash-Dot-Dot.

- **Antialiasing Enabled/Disabled**—Enabling this option smooths the edges of the shape outline/fill; disabling creates a more jagged edge.

- **Blend Mode**—Applies a blend mode to the shape outline/fill.

Chapter Conclusion

This chapter certainly covered a lot of ground, and by now it's probably clear how capable Paint.NET's tools are.

Here's what was covered:

- Accessing the Tools
- The Selection Tools
- The Move Tools
- The View Tools
- The Fill Tools
- The Drawing Tools
- The Photo Tools
- The Text and Shape Tools

Now that you've had a solid introduction to Paint.NET, let's move on to the next chapter and start doing some actual work!

CHAPTER 4

Correcting Tonality, Contrast, and Exposure

Now that we've taken the grand tour of Paint.NET's features and tools, it's time to do some actual work. In this chapter, we'll cover several techniques for making improvements in images that are too dark, dull, or have exposure issues that require adjustment.

The topics and tutorials covered in this chapter are

- An Overview of Image Tonality

- Tutorial 1: Correcting Exposure Using the Auto-Level Adjustment

- Tutorial 2: Correcting Exposure Using the Brightness/Contrast Adjustment

- A Look at BoltBait's Combined Adjustments Dialog

- Understanding the Curves Adjustments

- Tutorial 3: Correcting Dull Contrast Using the Curves Adjustment

- Tutorial 4: Minor Tonal Correction Using Curves

- Understanding the Levels Adjustment

- Tutorial 5: Correcting Underexposure Using the Levels Adjustment

- Correcting Local Tonality

- Tutorial 6: Darkening a Light Area

- Tutorial 7: Correcting Mixed Areas

- Chapter Conclusion

An Overview of Image Tonality

For the purposes of the tutorials in this book, image tonality refers to the quality of lightness values displayed in an image. Lightness values are measured in 256° that range on a scale from 0 (black) to 255 (white). The values in between are shades of gray.

The graphic in Figure 4-1 shows examples of highlights (light areas), midtones, and shadows (dark areas).

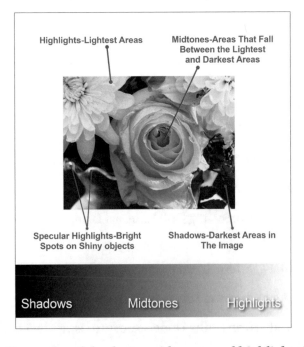

Figure 4-1. *Examples of shadows, midtones, and highlights in the image*

Tonal problems can result from a number of factors. Incorrect exposure (such as images that are too dark due to insufficient lighting) is one example. Also, prolonged exposure to light or chemical degradation (causing older photographic prints to fade) is another example.

Paint.NET is a great program for making tonal corrections in images; some images can be corrected with a single click, while others require manual adjustment. We'll look at several methods of correcting tonality in the upcoming tutorials.

Note   Images can sometimes benefit from a slight amount of sharpening. In many of the tutorials involving photographic images, that will be the last step—in most cases, using the default setting.

TUTORIAL 1: CORRECTING EXPOSURE USING THE AUTO-LEVEL ADJUSTMENT

The Auto-Level command equalizes the range of colors in an image; it makes automatic color and tonal corrections in digital photos. In this lesson, we'll use the Auto-Level adjustment to quickly correct an underexposed image:

1. Open the practice image *Ch4_Auto_Level_Fix* in Paint.NET.

2. Duplicate the Background layer by clicking the Duplicate Layer tab at the bottom of the Layers Window (Figure 4-2).

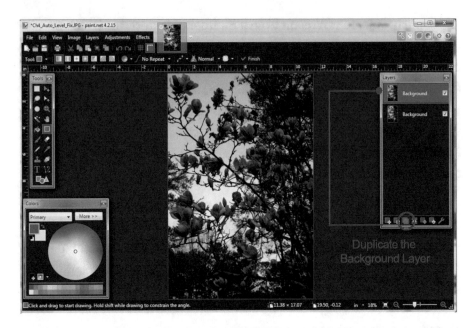

Figure 4-2. *Duplicate the Background layer by clicking the Duplicate Layer tab*

3. Double-click the duplicate layer's preview thumbnail to launch the Layer Properties dialog; rename the layer *Exposure Fix*, or something similar—then click OK.

4. Invoke the *Auto-Level command* (Adjustments ➤ Auto-Level).

5. Sharpen the image slightly (Effects ➤ Photo ➤ Sharpen); set the amount to 2, then click OK.

The image is noticeably brighter, as seen in Figure 4-3; when done, save the work as a pdn file (Paint.NET's native file format) or close it out.

Figure 4-3. *The before and after comparison*

Note   Although the Auto-Level command is fast and convenient, it may not always yield the desired result (or the best possible result). If the effect is too strong, it can be counteracted by lowering the layer opacity. If the effect isn't strong enough, then a more precise means of adjustment such as Curves or Levels will be required.

TUTORIAL 2: CORRECTING EXPOSURE USING THE BRIGHTNESS/CONTRAST ADJUSTMENT

In this lesson, we'll use the Brightness/Contrast adjustment to restore contrast in a dull image. As we saw in the previous lesson, Auto-Level is a one-click operation, but Brightness/Contrast offers a bit more control:

1. Open the practice image *Ch4_Brightness-Contrast_Fix* in Paint.NET.

2. Duplicate the Background layer by clicking the Duplicate Layer tab at the bottom of the Layers Window.

3. Double-click the duplicate layer's preview thumbnail to launch the Layer Properties dialog; rename the layer *Contrast Fix*, or something similar—then click OK.

4. Launch the *Brightness/Contrast dialog* (Adjustments ➤ Brightness/Contrast).

5. Move the Brightness slider to 8, then move the Contrast slider to 38—click OK when done (Figure 4-4).

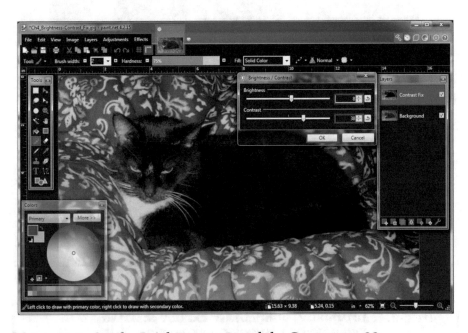

Figure 4-4. *Set the Brightness to 8 and the Contrast to 38*

6. Sharpen the image slightly (Effects ➤ Photo ➤ Sharpen); set the amount to 2, then click OK.

The image now has more contrast and "pops" more as seen in Figure 4-5; when done, save the work as a pdn file (Paint.NET's native file format) or close it out.

Note   Paint.NET will "remember" and retain these settings during the editing session until new settings are input, the settings are reset, or the program is closed.

Figure 4-5. *The before and after comparison*

Caution   The Brightness/Contrast dialog can be useful for making quick corrections in images with mild tonal issues. Because it lacks the precision of the more advanced *Curves* or *Levels* dialogs, it's easy to wipe out detail that appears in areas of shadow and highlights.

A Look at BoltBait's Combined Adjustments Dialog

If you installed BoltBait's Plugin Pack, there's a feature available shown called *Combined Adjustments* (Adjustments ➤ Combined Adjustments). This dialog features the Brightness/Contrast, Hue/Saturation/Lightness sliders, and a Color Conversion menu combined in a single window. Combined Adjustments allows minor adjustments to be made in brightness, contrast, and color. Figure 4-6 shows an old photograph from the 1970s undergoing minor contrast and color adjustments.

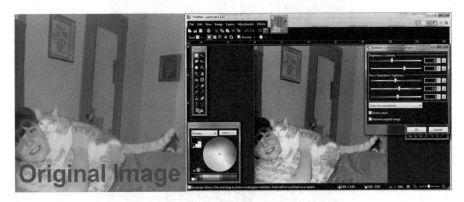

Figure 4-6. *BoltBait's Combined Adjustments dialog allows minor adjustments in Brightness/Contrast, Hue/Saturation/Lightness, and Color Conversion*

The Color Conversion menu offers a color to sepia command (Figure 4-7), as well as six colors to black and white conversions. We'll look closer at working with color in a later chapter.

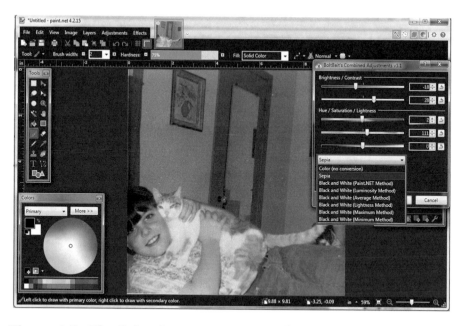

Figure 4-7. *The Color Conversion menu offers a command for converting color to sepia, as well as six methods of color to black and white conversion*

Understanding the Curves Adjustment Dialog

The Curves Adjustment is a powerful tool that's found in professional image editing software and is capable of precision tonal and color correction. For beginners, it usually takes some time and practice to use proficiently, but it's well worth the effort.

The Curves Adjustment dialog (Figure 4-8) is a graph with a line running diagonally from the lower-left corner of the graph to the upper-right corner. Adjustments in the left half of the graph affect the darkest range of pixels in the image, while adjustments in the right half affect the lightest. *Control Points* are placed along the line by clicking it; adjustments are made by dragging the line to form a curve, thus affecting the tone. Control Points can be removed by right-clicking them.

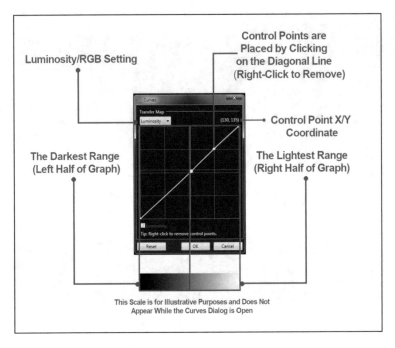

Figure 4-8. *The Curves Adjustment dialog*

The Curves Adjustment allows the user to make precision adjustments within ranges of tone. While the Brightness/Contrast Adjustment affects the pixels across the entire tonal range, Curves allows you to adjust a specific tonal range. In the example shown in Figure 4-9, the shadows in the image are lightened with more precision than the Brightness/Contrast dialog is capable of.

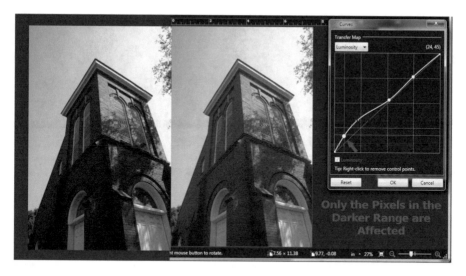

Figure 4-9. *The Curves Adjustment dialog is capable of precise tonal corrections*

Note   There's a tutorial a little later in this chapter using a different image, but a similar tonal problem as shown in the previous figure.

RGB Channel Adjustments

By default, the Curves Adjustment adjusts the Luminosity of the composite image, which includes the Red, Green, and Blue collectively. Adjustments can also be made to individual color channels. Figure 4-10 shows adjustments being made in the individual color channels, reducing the blue color cast. This is useful for precise color correction, which will be covered in a later chapter.

Figure 4-10. *Adjusting the color channels individually reduces the color cast in this image*

TUTORIAL 3: CORRECTING DULL CONTRAST USING THE CURVES ADJUSTMENT

In this lesson, we'll use the Curves Adjustment dialog to restore contrast in a dull image. As we saw in the previous lesson, the Brightness/Contrast was used; it should be apparent in this lesson how using Curves offers more control:

1. Open the practice image *Ch4_Curves-Contrast_Fix* in Paint.NET.

2. Duplicate the Background layer by clicking the Duplicate Layer tab at the bottom of the Layers Window.

3. Double-click the duplicate layer's preview thumbnail to launch the Layer Properties dialog; rename the layer *Contrast Fix*, or something similar—then click OK.

4. Open the *Curves Adjustment dialog* (Adjustments ➤ Curves); make sure it's set to *Luminosity*.

5. Using Figure 4-11 as a reference, place and position Control Points along the line to form a slight "S" shape to restore contrast—click OK when done.

Note   Hovering the cursor over a Control Point displays its X/Y coordinate in the upper-right corner of the Curves dialog. The X/Y coordinate of each Control Point is shown in the figure to help approximate the curve shape as closely as possible.

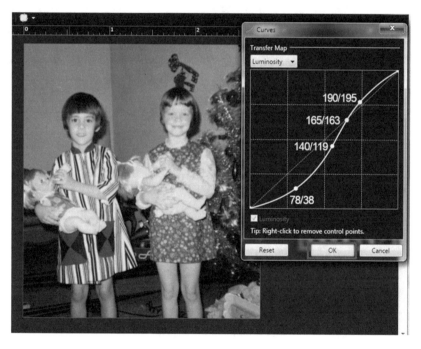

Figure 4-11. *Forming a slight "S" curve restores the contrast in this image*

6. Sharpen the image slightly (Effects ➤ Photo ➤ Sharpen); set the amount to 3, then click OK.

The image now has more contrast and "pops" more as seen in Figure 4-12; when done, save the work as a pdn file (Paint.NET's native file format) or close it out.

Figure 4-12. *The before and after comparison*

TUTORIAL 4: MINOR TONAL CORRECTION USING THE CURVES ADJUSTMENT

In this lesson, we'll use the Curves Adjustment dialog to make a minor tonal correction in a vertical view of a castle wall:

1. Open the practice image *Ch4_Curves_Tonal_Fix* in Paint.NET.

2. Duplicate the Background layer by clicking the Duplicate Layer tab at the bottom of the Layers Window.

3. Double-click the duplicate layer's preview thumbnail to launch the Layer Properties dialog; rename the layer *Tonal Fix*, or something similar—then click OK.

4. Open the *Curves Adjustment dialog* (Adjustments ➤ Curves); make sure it's set to *Luminosity*—if necessary, click *Reset* to restore the dialog to the default settings.

5. Using Figure 4-13 as a reference, place and position Control
    Points along the line to approximate (the X/Y coordinates are
    shown) the configuration shown—click OK when done.

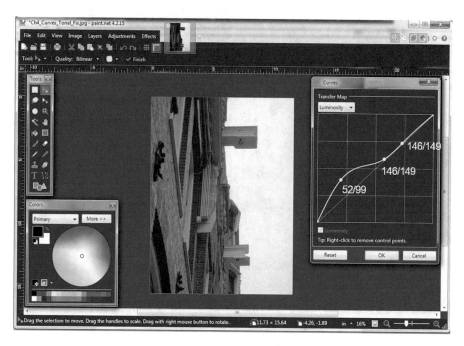

Figure 4-13. *Making the adjustment shown reveals detail in the
shadow areas while preserving the highlights and midtones*

6. Sharpen the image slightly (Effects ➤ Photo ➤ Sharpen); set
    the amount to 2, then click OK.

The wall now has more of its detail revealed as seen in Figure 4-14;
when done, save the work as a pdn file (Paint.NET's native file format) or
close it out.

Figure 4-14. *The before and after comparison*

Understanding the Levels Adjustment Dialog

The *Levels Adjustment* is another powerful tool that's capable of making tonal and color adjustments. Levels are used to alter the exposure of an image by remapping the input white (brightest pixels), black (darkest pixels), and gray points.

Figure 4-15 shows a breakdown of the Levels Adjustment dialog features.

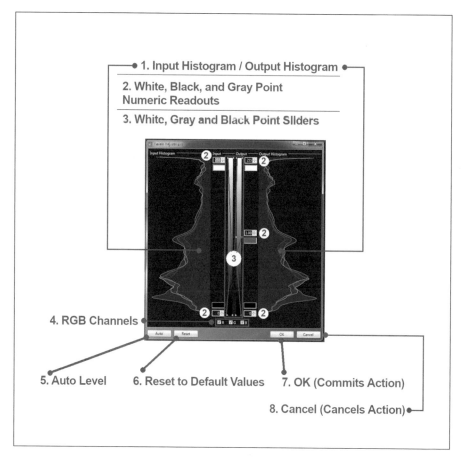

Figure 4-15. *The Levels Adjustment dialog*

The features of the Levels Adjustment dialog are as follows:

1. **Input Histogram/Output Histogram**—The *Input Histogram* displays tonal information of the image; when changes are made by moving the white, black, and gray point sliders, they are reflected in the *Output Histogram.*

2. **White, Black, and Gray Point Numeric Readout/ Input Boxes**—Displays the level of pixel brightness that corresponds with the white, black, or gray point sliders; by double-clicking in the boxes, numeric values can be input manually (the changes won't be apparent until the OK button is clicked).

3. **White, Black, and Gray Point Sliders**—Changes the white, black, or gray points of the image.

4. **RGB Channels**—When all three boxes are checked, adjusting the Levels affects the red, green, and blue channels collectively; unchecking a box leaves that color channel unaffected when changes are made.

5. **Auto Level**—Adjusts the Levels automatically; can also be done without launching the Levels Adjustment dialog (Adjustments ➤ Auto Level).

6. **Reset**—Reverts to the default settings.

7. **OK**—Commits the action.

8. **Cancel**—Cancels the action.

The Histogram

The Levels Adjustment displays a *histogram* (two, actually) that is a graphical representation of the tonal information in an image. This tonal information is displayed in each color channel. When an image has good tonal range, the graph spans the entire length (or at least, most of it). The example in Figure 4-16 shows an image with good tonal range.

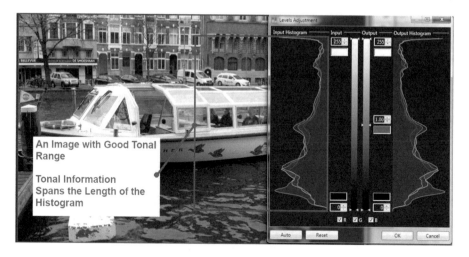

Figure 4-16. *This is an example of a good tonal range; the tonal information spans the length of the histogram*

Using the same image that was in Tutorial 2, we'll see how the contrast is corrected using Levels (Figure 4-17). The gaps in the Input Histogram indicate a lack of brightness in the highlights tonal range and, to a lesser degree, darkness in the shadow tonal range, resulting in dull highlights and muddy shadows in the image. By adjusting the White, Black, and Gray Point sliders, the tonality is remapped. The resulting changes are shown in the Output Histogram.

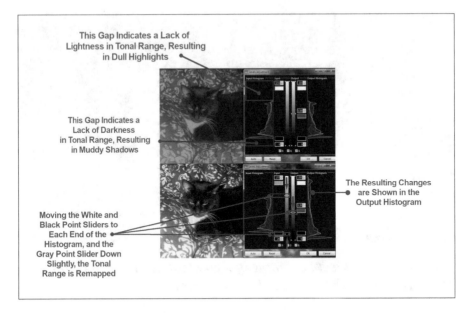

Figure 4-17. *By adjusting the White, Black, and Gray Points in the Levels Adjustment dialog, the tonality is remapped and the changes are shown in the Output Histogram*

TUTORIAL 5: CORRECTING UNDEREXPOSURE USING THE LEVELS ADJUSTMENT

In this lesson, we'll use the Levels Adjustment dialog to correct an underexposed (dark) image:

1. Open the practice image *Ch4_Levels_Underexposure_Fix* in Paint.NET.

2. Duplicate the Background layer by clicking the Duplicate Layer tab at the bottom of the Layers Window.

3. Double-click the duplicate layer's preview thumbnail to launch the Layer Properties dialog; rename the layer *Exposure Fix* or something similar, then click OK.

4.   Open the *Levels Adjustment dialog* (Adjustments ➤ Levels);
     if necessary, click *Reset* to restore the dialog to the default
     settings.

5.   Using Figure 4-18 as a reference, move the White Point slider
     down as shown (the input value should read 116), and move
     the Gray Point slider up (the input value should read 0.90)—
     click OK when done.

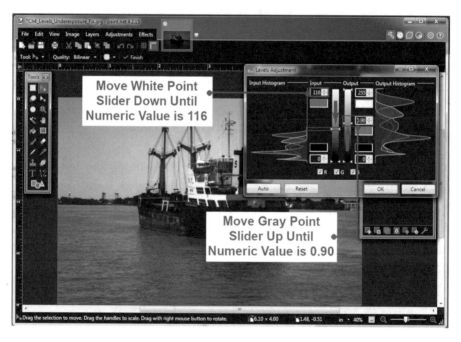

Figure 4-18. *Move the White Point and Gray Point sliders as shown
to remap the tonal range*

6.   Sharpen the image slightly (Effects ➤ Photo ➤ Sharpen); set
     the amount to 2, then click OK.

The photo is now much brighter, as seen in Figure 4-19; when done, save the work as a pdn file (Paint.NET's native file format) or close it out.

Figure 4-19. *The before and after comparison*

Correcting Local Tonality

Local tonality refers to an image that requires adjustment only in certain areas. In other image editing programs, this is usually accomplished using the *Dodge* and *Burn* tools; these are not included in Paint.NET (there is a plugin available that adds the Dodge and Burn tools that's discussed in the Appendix). The Dodge tool is used to lighten an area, while the Burn tool is used to darken an area.

There are techniques that produce similar results as the Dodge and Burn tools that don't require the addition of plugins.

TUTORIAL 6: DARKENING A LIGHT AREA

In this lesson, we'll use the Paintbrush Tool in combination with a layer set to the Soft Light blend mode to darken overexposed areas in an image:

1. Open the practice image *Ch4_Darken_Light_Area* in Paint.NET.

2. Duplicate the Background layer by clicking the Duplicate Layer tab at the bottom of the Layers Window.

3. Add a new layer by clicking the Add New Layer tab at the bottom of the Layers Window.

4. Double-click the new layer to open the Layer Properties dialog.

5. Name the layer Darken, and change the blend mode to *Overlay* (Figure 4-20)—click OK when done.

Figure 4-20. *Name the new layer Darken and change the blend mode to Overlay*

6. Change the Primary Color to dark gray—click the More button to expand the Colors Window and set the RGB values to 64 (on each channel) as shown in Figure 4-21.

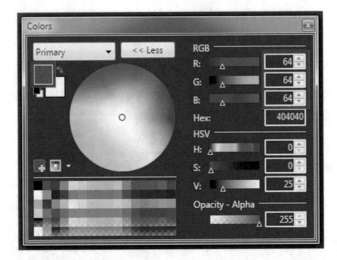

Figure 4-21. *Change the Primary Color to dark gray using the numeric values shown*

7. Select the Paintbrush Tool (B); change the width to about 100 pixels, and set the hardness to 0.

8. Brush along the foreground, avoiding the shadow areas indicated in Figure 4-22—reduce the brush size as needed when working around the shadows.

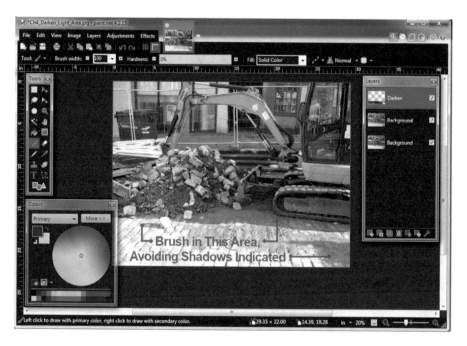

Figure 4-22. *Brush in the foreground area, avoiding the shadows indicated*

9. Add a new layer by clicking the Add New Layer tab at the bottom of the Layers Window.

10. Double-click the new layer to open the Layer Properties dialog.

11. Name the layer Darken, and change the blend mode to *Overlay*; lower the layer's opacity to 128 (Figure 4-23)—click OK when done.

Figure 4-23. *Set the layer properties as shown*

12. Select the Paintbrush Tool (B); change the width to about 40 pixels, and set the hardness to 0.

13. Zoom in and brush in the smallest areas in the shadows, then expand outward—increase the brush size as needed (Figure 4-24).

Figure 4-24. *Brush in the shadow areas indicated*

14. Click the Merge Layer Down tab in the Layers Window.

15. Merge the layer named Shadows down on the layer named Darken (these will now become one layer)—click again and merge to the duplicate background layer.

16. Sharpen the image slightly (Effects ➤ Photo ➤ Sharpen); set the amount to 2, then click OK.

Figure 4-25 shows the before and after result—note the foreground is a bit less washed out and has more contrast. When done, save the work as a pdn file (Paint.NET's native file format) or close it out.

Figure 4-25. *The before and after comparison*

TUTORIAL 7: CORRECTING MIXED AREAS

In this lesson, we'll use the Paintbrush Tool in combination with a layer set to the Soft Light blend mode to lighten a large, dark area and lighten some other smaller ones in an image:

1. Open the practice image *Ch4_Lighten_Dark_Area* in Paint.NET.

2. Duplicate the Background layer by clicking the Duplicate Layer.

3. Add a new layer by clicking the Add New Layer tab at the bottom of the Layers Window.

4. Double-click the new layer to open the Layer Properties dialog.

5. Name the layer Lighten Fur, and change the blend mode to *Overlay*; lower the layer's opacity to 180 (Figure 4-26)—click OK when done.

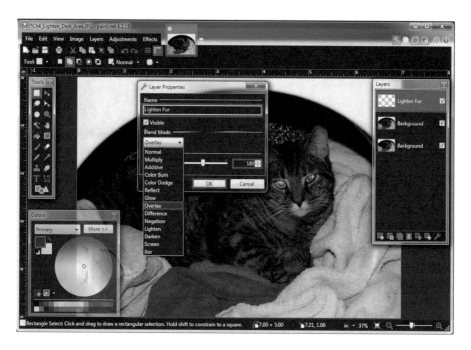

Figure 4-26. *Set the layer properties as shown*

6. Change the Primary Color to white.

7. Select the Paintbrush Tool (B); change the width to about 150 pixels, and set the hardness to 0.

8. Brush along the cat's fur to lighten it, avoiding the facial areas indicated in Figure 4-27—reduce the brush size as needed when working around the face.

Figure 4-27. *Brush along the fur, excluding the areas indicated*

9. Add a new layer by clicking the Add New Layer tab at the bottom of the Layers Window.

10. Double-click the new layer to open the Layer Properties dialog.

11. Name the layer *Eyes*, and change the blend mode to *Overlay*, lower the layer's opacity to 128—click OK when done.

12. Change the Primary Color to black.

13. Select the Paintbrush Tool (B); change the width to about 18–19 pixels, and set the hardness to 0.

14. Brush in the cat's eyes to reduce the reflection and darken the iris (Figure 4-28).

Figure 4-28. *Brush in the eyes to darken*

15. Add a new layer by clicking the Add New Layer tab at the bottom of the Layers Window.

16. Double-click the new layer to open the Layer Properties dialog.

17. Name the layer *Ears-Mouth*, and change the blend mode to *Overlay*, lower the layer's opacity to 90—click OK when done.

18. Change the Primary Color to white.

19. Select the Paintbrush Tool (B); change the width to about 30.

20. Brush in the ears and the white area around the mouth to lighten slightly (Figure 4-29).

Figure 4-29. *Brush in the ears and around the mouth to lighten slightly*

21. Click the duplicate Background Layer to make it active.

22. Sharpen the image slightly (Effects ➤ Photo ➤ Sharpen); set the amount to 1, then click OK.

Figure 4-30 shows the before and after result—note the cat's fur is lighter, shows more detail, and the eyes are less reflective. When done, save the work as a pdn file (Paint.NET's native file format) or close it out.

Figure 4-30. *The before and after comparison*

Chapter Conclusion

We covered a lot in this chapter, and if you're a beginner to image editing, you learned much about tonality and how to fix common related issues.

Here's a recap of what was covered:

- An Overview of Image Tonality

- Correcting Exposure Using the Auto-Level Adjustment

- Correcting Exposure Using the Brightness/Contrast Adjustment

- A Look at BoltBait's Combined Adjustments Dialog

- Understanding the Curves Adjustments

- Correcting Dull Contrast Using the Curves Adjustment

- Minor Tonal Correction Using Curves

- Understanding the Levels Adjustment

- Correcting Underexposure Using the Levels Adjustment

- Correcting Local Tonality

- Darkening a Light Area

- Correcting Mixed Areas

In the next chapter, we'll learn how to correct color problems using Paint.NET.

CHAPTER 5

Enhancing, Correcting, and Working with Color

Now that we've learned about adjusting and correcting contrast and other tonal issues, we'll look at correcting color problems, as well as other aspects of working with color.

The topics and tutorials covered in this chapter are

- An Overview of Color Problems

- Tutorial 8: Reviving a Faded Color Photo Using Levels

- Tutorial 9: Correcting Color Using Curves

- Tutorial 10: Color Correction Using Color Balance (BoltBait's Plugin Pack Required)

- Tutorial 11: Turning a Color Photo into Black and White (BoltBait's Plugin Pack Required)

- Tutorial 12: Using the Sepia Adjustment

- Tutorial 13: Colorizing a Black and White Photo

- Chapter Conclusion

© Phillip Whitt 2022
P. Whitt, *Practical Paint.NET*, https://doi.org/10.1007/978-1-4842-7283-1_5

An Overview of Color Problems

Photographs can have color problems for a variety of reasons. Older color prints may fade, or the dyes may shift over time. Figure 5-1 shows an old color photograph taken in 1966 that has undergone a loss of color (particularly, the magenta dye in the print's emulsion has all but faded away). You'll work with an image similar to this one a little later to drastically improve it.

Figure 5-1. *This old color photograph with severe color loss*

Digital photos may have a color cast (a preponderance of one color) due to an improper white balance setting. Figure 5-2 shows an image with a magenta color cast (another one you'll work on a little later in this chapter).

Figure 5-2. *This image has a magenta color cast*

TUTORIAL 8: REVIVING A FADED COLOR PHOTO USING LEVELS

In this tutorial, we're going to improve the old color photograph that was discussed earlier using Levels:

1. Open the practice image *Ch5_Faded_Color_Fix* in Paint.NET.

2. Duplicate the Background layer by clicking the Duplicate Layer tab at the bottom of the Layers Window.

3. Double-click the duplicate layer's preview thumbnail to launch the Layer Properties dialog; rename the layer *Faded Color Fix*, or something similar—then click OK.

4. Open the Levels Adjustment dialog (Adjustments ➤ Levels)—if necessary, click Reset to restore the dialog to the default settings.

5. Disable the green and blue color channels by unchecking their respective boxes, leaving the red color channel active (Figure 5-3).

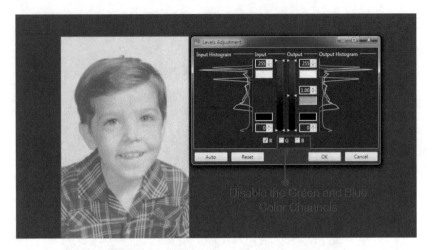

Figure 5-3. *Disable the green and blue color channels*

6. On the *Input Histogram* side of the Levels Adjustment,
   move the white point (top) slider down until the numeric
   readout is 235—this is about where the graph representing the
   lighter image data begins for the red channel (Figure 5-4).

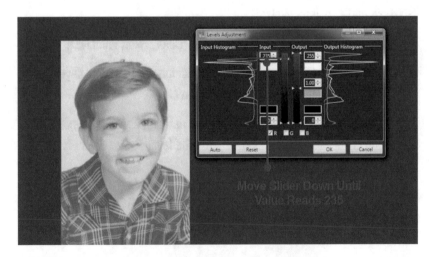

Figure 5-4. *Move the slider until the readout is 235*

7. Now, make sure the *red* and *blue* channels are disabled and *make the green color channel active*—move the white and black point sliders toward the image data shown in the graph for the green channel until the numeric readouts are 229 and 84 (Figure 5-5).

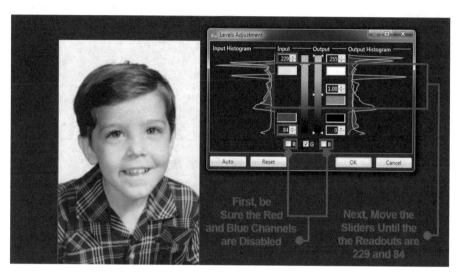

Figure 5-5. *Make the adjustments shown to the green color channel*

8. Now, make sure the *red* and *green* channels are disabled and *make the blue color channel active*—move the white and black point sliders toward the image data shown in the graph for the blue channel until the numeric readouts are 191 and 63 (Figure 5-6), then click OK.

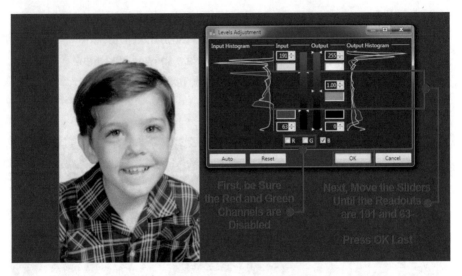

Figure 5-6. *Make the adjustments shown to the blue color channel*

9. Sharpen the image slightly (Effects ➤ Photo ➤ Sharpen); set the amount to 2, then click OK.

Using the Levels Adjustment allowed the image data of each color channel to be remapped independently, resulting in a vastly improved image (Figure 5-7). When done, save the work as a pdn file (Paint.NET's native file format) or close it out.

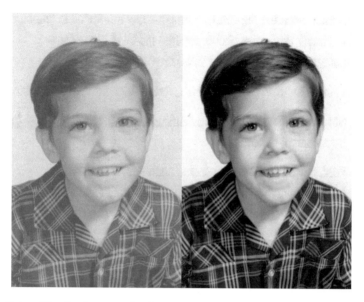

Figure 5-7. *The before and after comparison*

Note   Even though this image ended up with good results, some photos with severe color loss may be improved, but still need more work than using the Levels Adjustment by itself can completely fix.

TUTORIAL 9: COLOR CORRECTION USING CURVES

In this lesson, we'll use the Curves Adjustment dialog to correct a blue color cast in a digital photo. We'll also use the *Gradient Tool* in combination with a layer *blend mode* to make the sky a deeper blue:

1. Open the practice image *Ch5_Curves_Color_Correction* in Paint.NET.

2. Duplicate the Background layer by clicking the Duplicate Layer tab at the bottom of the Layers Window.

3. Double-click the duplicate layer's preview thumbnail to launch the Layer Properties dialog; rename the layer *Color Fix*, or something similar—then click OK.

4. Launch the *Curves Adjustments dialog* (Adjustments ➤ Curves).

5. Set the *Transfer Map* to RGB—this allows each color channel to be adjusted individually.

6. First, disable the *green* and *blue* channels, then move the line (adjusting the red channel) to the grid area shown in Figure 5-8—the approximate X/Y coordinates should be 96/158.

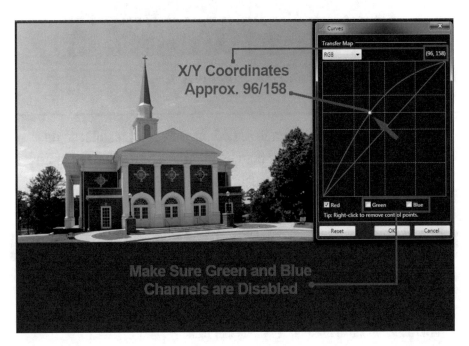

Figure 5-8. *Make the adjustment shown to the red color channel*

7. Next, make sure the *red* and *blue* channels are disabled, and *make the green channel active;* move the line *just slightly* to the grid area to the approximate X/Y coordinates shown in Figure 5-9.

Figure 5-9. *Make the adjustment shown to the green color channel*

8. Next, make sure the *red* and *green* channels are disabled, and *make the blue channel active;* move the line to the grid area to the approximate X/Y coordinates shown in Figure 5-10, then click OK.

Figure 5-10. *Make the adjustment shown to the blue color channel, then click OK*

9. Sharpen the image slightly (Effects ➤ Photo ➤ Sharpen); set the amount to 2, then click OK.

10. Now, the color has been balanced and the image looks much better, but let's add a finishing touch to further enhance it by making the sky a deeper blue; duplicate the layer named *Color Fix* (or whatever name you gave it) by clicking the Duplicate Layer tab at the bottom of the Layers Window.

11. Double-click the layer preview thumbnail image to open the *Layer Properties* dialog—change the blend mode to Multiply, then click OK (Figure 5-11).

Figure 5-11. *Set the blend mode to Multiply*

12. Make sure the Primary Color is set to Black.

13. Select the *Gradient Tool* (G); with the tool set to *Linear* and
    Transparency Mode, click and drag about 60% of the way down
    as shown in Figure 5-12 and press Enter to finish the gradient.

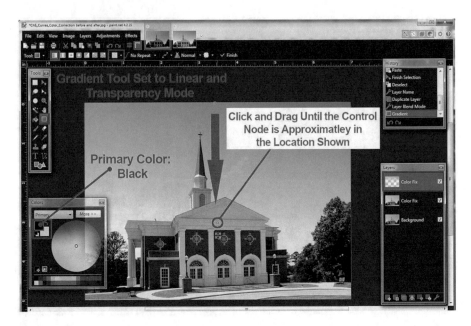

Figure 5-12. *Drawing a gradient with the settings shown makes the sky a deeper blue*

Using the Curves Adjustment allowed each color channel to be adjusted independently, offsetting the color cast for an improved image. Using the Gradient Tool in combination with a layer set to the Multiply Blend Mode, the sky was given a deeper blue (Figure 5-13). When done, save the work as a pdn file (Paint.NET's native file format) or close it out.

Figure 5-13. *The before and after comparison*

TUTORIAL 10: COLOR CORRECTION USING COLOR BALANCE (BOLTBAIT'S PLUGIN PACK REQUIRED)

Some color issues can be more easily and quickly corrected using other means. In this lesson, we'll use the Color Balance Adjustment dialog to correct a magenta color cast in a digital photo (this requires the installation of BoltBait's Plugin Pack covered in Chapter 1):

1. Open the practice image *Ch5_Color_Balance* in Paint.NET.

2. Duplicate the Background layer by clicking the Duplicate Layer tab at the bottom of the Layers Window.

3. Open the *Color Balance* dialog (Adjustments ➤ Color Balance).

4. Move the Magenta/Green slider to the right until the setting is on 20, move the Yellow/Blue slider to the right until the setting is –5, and move the Contrast slider to the right until the setting is 20 (Figure 5-14)—click OK when done.

Figure 5-14. *Use the settings shown to offset the color cast and boost the contrast slightly*

5. Sharpen the image slightly (Effects ➤ Photo ➤ Sharpen); set the amount to 3, then click OK (this image was shot through a glass window, so it isn't as crisp as it might have otherwise been).

Using BoltBait's Color Adjustment offers a quick and easy way to correct color casts as seen in Figure 5-15 (although Curves is usually more precise). When done, save the work as a pdn file (Paint.NET's native file format) or close it out.

Figure 5-15. *The before and after comparison*

TUTORIAL 11: TURNING A COLOR PHOTO INTO BLACK AND WHITE (BOLTBAIT'S PLUGIN PACK REQUIRED)

In this tutorial, we'll turn a color photograph to black and white using the *Black and White +* plugin by BoltBait. Paint.NET *does* have a native Black and White adjustment (Figure 5-16), but it is a one-click operation with no options for adjusting the result, other than using another adjustment such as Curves afterward. The Black and White + plugin offers a choice of preset options with Brightness-Contrast sliders. This allows quick color to black and white conversions, with some latitude for adjusting the result.

Figure 5-16. *Paint.NET's one-click Black and White Adjustment*

1. Open the practice image *Ch5_Color_to_Black_and_White* in Paint.NET.

2. Duplicate the Background layer by clicking the Duplicate Layer tab at the bottom of the Layers Window—rename the layer *Black and White* (or something similar).

3. Open BoltBait's *Black and White +* dialog (Adjustments ➤ Black and White)—see Figure 5-17.

Figure 5-17. *BoltBait's Black and White + plugin*

4. As shown in Figure 5-18, select the *Average Method* setting, and increase the Brightness to 4, and decrease the Contrast to 10.

Figure 5-18. *Using the Average Method with slight adjustments in Brightness and Contrast*

Using BoltBait's Black and White + Adjustment offers some latitude when adjusting images that have been converted to Black and White—Figure 5-19 shows the before and after comparison. When done, save the work as a pdn file (Paint.NET's native file format) or close it out.

Figure 5-19. *The before and after comparison*

BoltBait's Black and White + plugin has six presets:

- Paint.NET Method
- Luminosity Method
- Average Method
- Lightness Method
- Maximum Method
- Minimum Method

Figure 5-20 shows a comparison—there's only a slight difference between the Paint.NET, Luminosity, and Average methods, but the Lightness, Maximum, and Minimum methods are more noticeable.

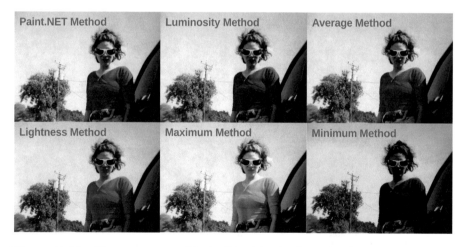

Figure 5-20. *The presets used in BoltBait's Black and White + plugin*

Note   The G'MIC-Qt plugin for Paint.NET offers a wide variety of filters—among them is a filter for black and white conversions that offers even more control for fine-tuning the results. The G'MIC-Qt plugin will be covered in the Appendix of this book.

TUTORIAL 12: USING THE SEPIA ADJUSTMENT

This is an easy lesson that you may find useful (and fun) in working with your own family photos.

In this tutorial, we'll crop a color contemporary image for better composition, then apply the Sepia Adjustment to give it an antique look:

1. Open the practice image *Ch5_Color_to_Sepia* in Paint.NET.

2. We'll now crop the image for better composition—using the *Rectangle Select Tool* (S), make a selection (approximate is okay) around the cabin as shown in Figure 5-21, then crop (Image ➤ Crop to Selection).

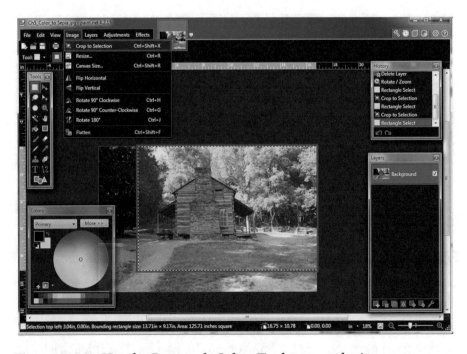

Figure 5-21. *Use the Rectangle Select Tool to crop the image as shown*

Note   Cropping the image in this manner utilizes (although somewhat roughly) the *Rule of Thirds*, which is essentially placing the subject off-center using a grid dividing the image into nine sections. There's a detailed tutorial about using the Rule of Thirds in a Paint.NET forum page that can be found here: `https://forums.getpaint.net/topic/12282-cropping-photographs-the-rule-of-thirds/`.

3. Duplicate the Background layer by clicking the Duplicate Layer tab at the bottom of the Layers Window—rename the layer *Sepia* (or something similar).

4. Apply the Sepia Adjustment as shown in Figure 5-22 (Adjustment ➤ Sepia).

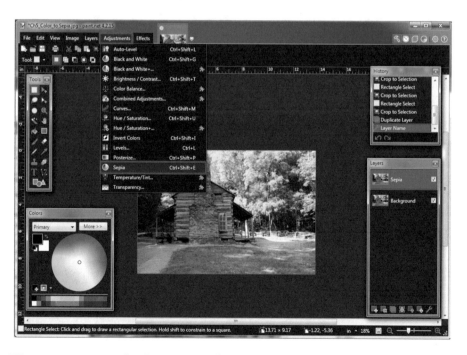

Figure 5-22.   *Apply the Sepia Adjustment*

5. Sharpen the image slightly (Effects ➤ Photo ➤ Sharpen); set
    the amount to 2, then click OK.

The Sepia Adjustment mimics the earth tone finish that was common
in older photographs from the late 19th and early 20th centuries. In the
before and after example (Figure 5-23), the sepia tone is a good fit for the
image of the log cabin. When done, save the work as a pdn file (Paint.NET's
native file format) or close it out.

Figure 5-23. *The before and after comparison*

By lowering the opacity of the layer the sepia effect was applied to,
some of the underlying color will show through, resulting in an image with
subtle color (Figure 5-24).

Figure 5-24. *Lower the layer opacity for subtle color*

TUTORIAL 13: COLORIZING A BLACK AND WHITE PHOTO

In this tutorial, we'll colorize an old black and white photo to give the image a hand-tinted look (the way photographs were colorized at one time):

1. Open the practice image *Ch5_Colorize* in Paint.NET.

2. Duplicate the Background layer by clicking the Duplicate Layer tab at the bottom of the Layers Window.

3. Using the *Lasso Select Tool* (S,S), draw a selection around the hair, face, and exposed flesh (Figure 5-25)—it should extend just a little outside the edges to make sure these areas are completely selected.

Figure 5-25. *Make a selection as shown using the Lasso Select Tool*

4.   Copy the selected area (Edit ➤ Copy).

5.   Paste into a new layer (Edit ➤ Paste into New Layer)—rename the layer *Flesh Tone* (or something similar).

6.   Open the Hue/Saturation dialog (Adjustments ➤ Hue/Saturation).

7.   Move the *Saturation* slider to the right until the numeric value is 150—click OK when done (Figure 5-26).

Figure 5-26. *Move the Saturation slider until the value reads 150, then click OK*

8. Using the Eraser Tool (E), set the brush width to about 50 pixels and the hardness to 50%—erase the excess color (vary the brush width and zoom in as needed) as shown in Figure 5-27.

Figure 5-27. *Use the Eraser Tool to remove the excess color, varying the brush width as needed*

9. Using the Lasso Tool (S,S), draw a selection around the hair as shown in Figure 5-28.

Figure 5-28. *Make a selection as shown using the Lasso Select Tool*

10. Copy the selected area (Edit ➤ Copy).

11. Paste into a new layer (Edit ➤ Paste into New Layer)—rename the layer *Hair*.

12. Now, we'll change the hair color a bit; open the Hue/Saturation dialog (Adjustments ➤ Hue/Saturation).

13. Move the *Hue* slider slightly to the right until the numeric value is 12—click OK when done (Figure 5-29).

Figure 5-29. *Move the Hue slider until the value reads 12, then click OK*

14. Set the Primary Color to red.

15. Add a new layer by clicking the *Add New Layer* tab on the bottom of the Layers Window.

16. Double-click the layer preview thumbnail to open the Layer Properties dialog—change the Blend Mode to *Overlay* and rename it *Cheeks*, then click OK.

17. Using the Paintbrush Tool (B), set the brush width to about 75 pixels and the hardness to 0—apply red to the cheeks as shown in Figure 5-30.

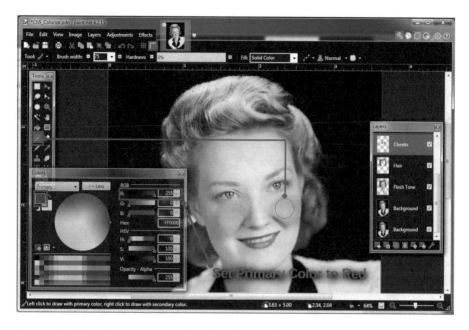

Figure 5-30. *Apply red to the cheeks as shown*

18.   Now, we'll give the cheeks just a hint of red—reopen the Layer
      Properties dialog and lower the layer opacity to 50 (Figure 5-31),
      then click OK.

Figure 5-31. *Lower the layer opacity to 50 for just a hint of red in the cheeks*

19. Add a new layer by clicking the *Add New Layer* tab on the bottom of the Layers Window.

20. Double-click the layer preview thumbnail to open the Layer Properties dialog—change the Blend Mode to *Overlay* and rename it *Lips*.

21. Lower the layer opacity to 70, then click OK.

22. Using the Paintbrush Tool (B), set the brush width to about 7 pixels and the hardness to 0—apply red to the lips as shown in Figure 5-32 (zoom in and adjust the brush width as needed).

23. Set the Primary Color to green.

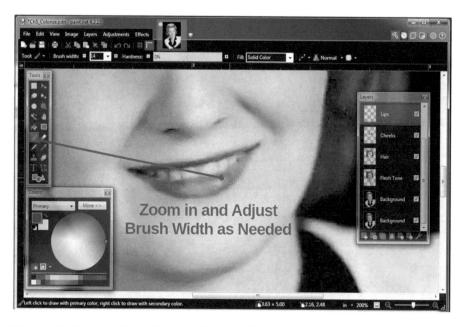

Figure 5-32. *Apply red to the lips as shown*

24. Add a new layer by clicking the *Add New Layer* tab on the bottom of the Layers Window.

25. Double-click the layer preview thumbnail to open the Layer Properties dialog—change the Blend Mode to Overlay and rename it *Eyes*.

26. Lower the layer opacity to 55, then click OK.

27. Using the Paintbrush Tool (B), set the brush width to about 15 pixels and the hardness to 0—apply green to the iris of each eye as shown in Figure 5-33 (zoom in and adjust the brush width as needed).

Figure 5-33. *Apply green to the iris of each eye as shown*

28. Set the Primary Color to white.

29. Add a new layer by clicking the *Add New Layer* tab on the
     bottom of the Layers Window.

30. Double-click the layer preview thumbnail to open the Layer
     Properties dialog—change the Blend Mode to Overlay and
     rename it *Teeth-Eye Whites*.

31. Lower the layer opacity to 80, then click OK.

32. Now we'll brighten the whites of the eyes and the teeth. Using
     the Paintbrush Tool (B), set the brush width to about 10 pixels
     and the hardness to 0—apply white to the white of each eye
     and the teeth as shown in Figure 5-34 (zoom in and adjust the
     brush width as needed).

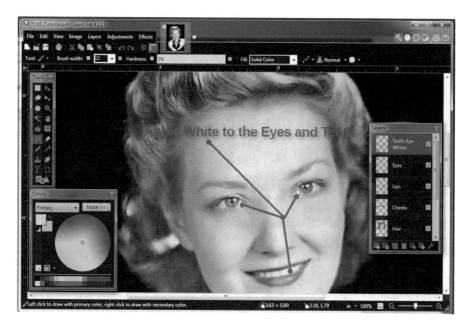

Figure 5-34. *Apply white to each eye (the eye whites only) and teeth as shown*

Color makes quite a difference (not necessarily better) as we can see in Figure 5-35. When done, save the work as a pdn file (Paint.NET's native file format) or close it out.

Figure 5-35. *Before and after comparison*

Chapter Conclusion

We covered a lot in this chapter and covered a great deal about working with color images.

Here's a recap of what was covered:

- An Overview of Color Problems

- Reviving a Faded Color Photo Using Levels

- Correcting Color Using Curves

- Color Correction Using Color Balance (BoltBait's Plugin Pack Required)

- Turning a Color Photo into Black and White (BoltBait's Plugin Pack Required)

- Using the Sepia Adjustment

- Colorizing a Black and White Photo

In the next chapter, we'll look at modifying, retouching, and restoring photographs.

CHAPTER 6

Modifying, Retouching, and Restoring Photos

In this chapter, we'll cover a basic alteration (in this case, removing unsightly power lines), as well as retouching images to brighten teeth and remove blemishes. We'll also cover restoring scratch and damaged images.

The tutorials covered in this chapter are

- Tutorial 14: Removing Unwanted Objects
- Tutorial 15: Straightening an Image
- Tutorial 16: Brightening Teeth
- Tutorial 17: Removing Blemishes
- Tutorial 18: Repairing Scratches and Damage
- Chapter Conclusion

© Phillip Whitt 2022
P. Whitt, *Practical Paint.NET*, https://doi.org/10.1007/978-1-4842-7283-1_6

TUTORIAL 14: REMOVING UNWANTED OBJECTS

In this tutorial, we're going to remove the power lines from a picture of an antique street lamp to make it more visually pleasing:

1. Open the practice image *Ch6_Old_Lamp*.

2. Duplicate the Background layer by clicking the Duplicate Layer tab at the bottom of the Layers Window.

3. Double-click the duplicate layer's preview thumbnail to launch the Layer Properties dialog; rename the layer *Clone* or something similar—then click OK.

4. Open the Clone Stamp Tool (L).

5. Set the Brush width to 6 pixels and the hardness to 50%; sample the pixels in a nearby area (Ctrl-click) and work around the lamp to start digitally removing the power lines (Figure 6-1).

Figure 6-1. *Start cloning around the lamp as shown*

6.   Continue cloning the areas next to the lamp as shown in
     Figure 6-2; sample nearby areas often (Ctrl-click).

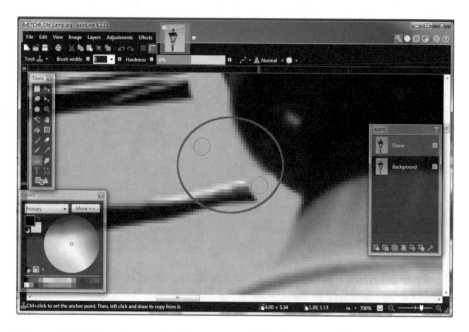

Figure 6-2. *Continue cloning around the lamp as shown*

7.   After the power lines around the lamp have been cloned out,
     work outward as shown in in Figure 6-3; increase the brush
     size as needed.

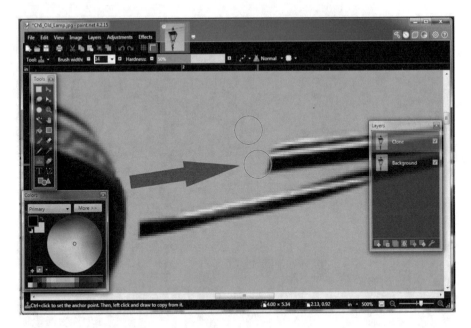

Figure 6-3. *After the areas around the lamp have been cloned,*
continue by working outward as shown

8. Lastly, we'll now remove the portions of the power lines visible
    through (and reflected off of) the glass panes of the lamp
    (Figure 6-4).

Figure 6-4. *The last thing to do is to remove the power lines visible through and reflected off of the glass panes of the lamp*

Using the Clone Stamp Tool, the power lines were digitally removed for a more visually appealing image as seen in Figure 6-5. When done, save the work as a pdn file (Paint.NET's native file format) or close it out.

Figure 6-5. *The before and after comparison*

TUTORIAL 15: STRAIGHTENING AN IMAGE

In this lesson, we'll use the Curves Adjustment dialog to correct a blue color cast in a digital photo. We'll also use the Gradient Tool in combination with a layer *blend mode* to make the sky a deeper blue:

1. Open the practice image *Ch6_Straighten_Building* in Paint.NET.

2. Duplicate the Background layer by clicking the Duplicate Layer tab at the bottom of the Layers Window.

3. Double-click the duplicate layer's preview thumbnail to launch the Layer Properties dialog; rename the layer *Straighten*, or something similar—then click OK.

4. It will be helpful to create a horizontal guide to help aid in straightening the building; create a new layer by clicking the Add New Layer tab at the bottom of the Layers Window.

5. Double-click the duplicate layer's preview thumbnail to launch the Layer Properties dialog; rename the layer *Guide*, or something similar—then click OK.

6. Click the Shapes Tool (O, O) in the Tools Window (it will be at the very bottom).

7. Select the Rectangle Shape; use the *Draw Filled Shape* and the *Fill: Solid Color* settings; in the Colors Window, set the Primary Color to a bright, easy-to-see color (Figure 6-6).

Figure 6-6. *Select the Rectangle Tool using the settings shown*

8. Draw a narrow, horizontal rectangle (on the layer named *Guide*) along the ledge of the building as shown in Figure 6-7; this guide provides a frame of reference that will help when making our upcoming adjustment.

Figure 6-7. *Using the Rectangle Tool draw a horizontal, narrow line as shown; this will serve as a guide*

9. Click the layer named *Straighten* to make it active.

10. Open the *Rotate/Zoom* menu (Layers ➤ Rotate/Zoom); move the Rotate slider slightly to the left until the numeric value reads −1.46 as shown in Figure 6-8 (it should snap to this setting when moving the slider very slightly), and click OK when done (if desired, you can discard the *Guide* layer after completing this step).

Figure 6-8. *Move the Rotate slider slightly to the left until the numeric value reads –1.46, then click OK*

Note   You may notice a slight upward bend in the ledge of the building; this is because of a slight camera lens distortion. For the purposes of this lesson, the main concern is that each end of the ledge aligns with the guide as much as possible.

---

11. After this layer has been straightened, the edges will be at a slight angle, revealing the pixels of the underlying layer; this will create a noticeable seam when examined closely—this can be more clearly demonstrated by hiding the background layer's visibility and revealing the transparent areas (Figure 6-9).

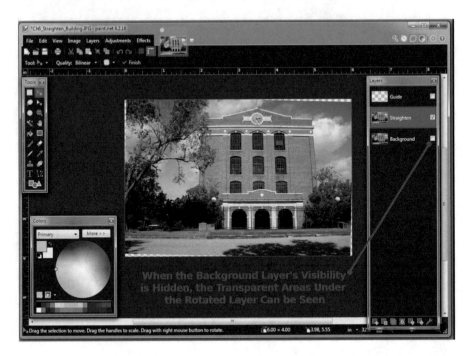

Figure 6-9. *The layer's edges are now at a slight angle after rotation; hiding the background layer's visibility demonstrates this more clearly*

12. To work around this issue, there are options available; the first is to slightly enlarge the layer using the *Rotate/Zoom* menu (Layers ➤ Rotate/Zoom)—move the zoom slider slightly to the right until the transparent areas are filled as shown in Figure 6-10 (the numeric value should be about 1.04), then click OK when done.

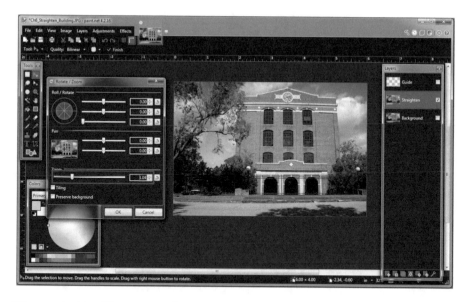

Figure 6-10. *The Rotate/Zoom menu can be used to slightly enlarge the rotated layer until the transparent areas are filled*

Note   While this method is easy, it may not always be the best one. In some images, it may cause important elements to be cropped out (notice how close the roof of the building is to the edge). The following steps will show an alternative that's a bit more labor intensive, but will preserve the important parts of the image.

---

13. For this step, undo Step 12 (Ctrl+Z); use the *Rectangle Select Tool* (S) to draw a selection as shown in Figure 6-11, then use the *Crop to Selection* option (this will crop out the transparent areas on the left, bottom, and right, but the top one will remain).

Figure 6-11. *Use the Rectangle Select Tool to make a selection as shown, then use the Crop to Selection option*

14. This action cropped the image, eliminating the transparent areas on the left, bottom, and right—because the building's roof is so close to the top edge, that was left intentionally to avoid cropping so close, leaving the transparent area on top of the image.

15. Select the *Clone Stamp* Tool (L); set the *Brush width* to 25 and the hardness to 0, then use it to fill in the transparent area (Figure 6-12).

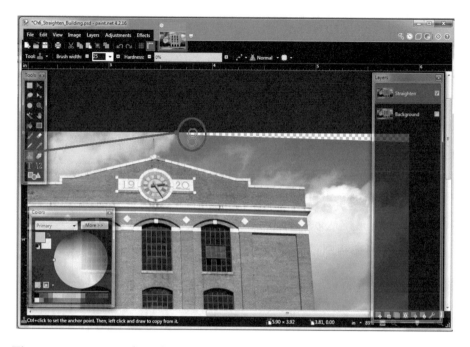

Figure 6-12. *Use the Clone Stamp Tool to fill in the transparent area*

Now the building looks much better, without so much tilt (Figure 6-13). When done, save the work as a pdn file (Paint.NET's native file format) or close it out.

Figure 6-13. *The before and after comparison*

TUTORIAL 16: BRIGHTENING TEETH

Paint.NET can be used for minor retouching projects on people to help make them look their best. In this lesson, we'll brighten a man's teeth just a bit (it will be a subtle improvement):

1. Open the practice image *Ch6_Brighten_Teeth* in Paint.NET.

2. Duplicate the Background layer by clicking the Duplicate Layer tab at the bottom of the Layers Window.

3. Using the *Lasso Select* Tool (S,S), draw a selection around the teeth as shown in Figure 6-14.

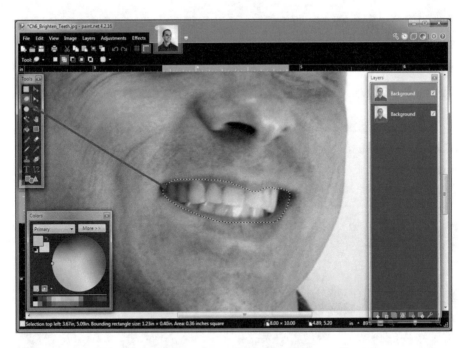

Figure 6-14. *Draw a selection around the teeth as shown*

4. Copy the selected area (Edit ➤ Copy).

5. Paste the copied selection into a new layer (Edit ➤ Paste into New Layer); deactivate the selection (Ctrl+D).

6. Rename the new layer Teeth or something similar.

7. Open the *Levels Adjustment* (Adjustments ➤ Levels).

8. Move the *Gray Point* (middle) slider until the numeric value reads about 0.72 as shown in Figure 6-15—click OK when done.

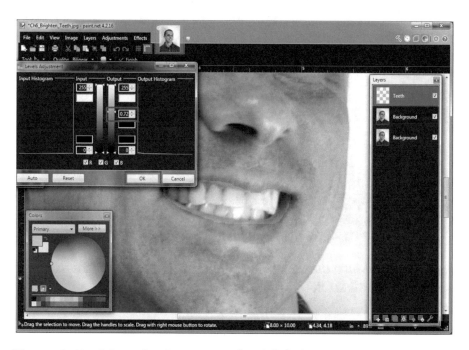

Figure 6-15. *Move the Gray Point (middle) slider until the numeric value reads 0.72, then click OK*

9. Open the *Hue/Saturation* dialog (Adjustments ➤ Hue/Saturation).

10.   Decrease the saturation slightly by moving the Saturation slider to the left until the numeric value reads 74 as shown in Figure 6-16, then click OK.

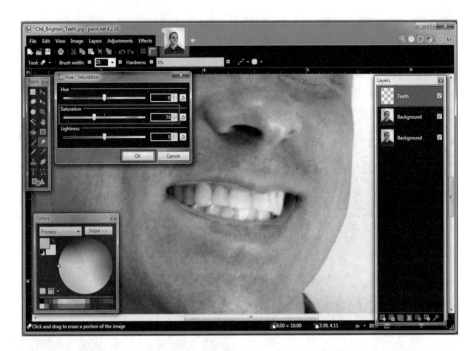

Figure 6-16. *Move the Saturation slider until the numeric value reads 74, then click OK*

11.   Using the *Eraser Tool* (E) with the hardness set to 0, remove the excess area around the teeth—adjust brush size as needed as you work (Figure 6-17).

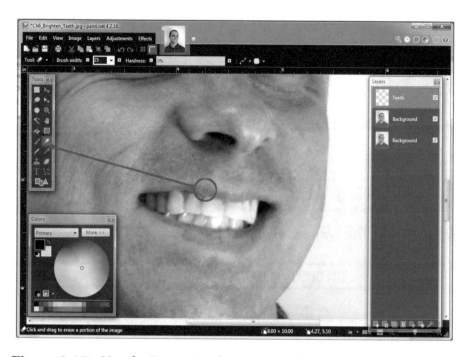

Figure 6-17. *Use the Eraser Tool to remove the excess area around the teeth*

The result is very subtle (Figure 6-18), but my goal was to enhance the teeth slightly while maintaining a natural look, and not end up with an overly "bleached" effect.

Note   Because the lightening effect on the teeth in this lesson is subtle, you can best see the result by toggling the visibility of the layer (named Teeth) on and off several times.

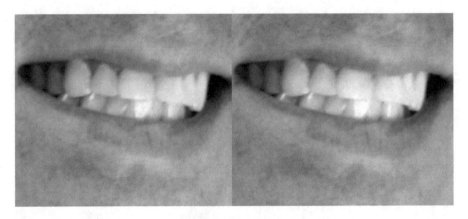

Figure 6-18. *The before and after comparison*

TUTORIAL 17: REMOVING BLEMISHES

In this tutorial, we'll use the Clone Stamp Tool to remove facial blemishes and age spots from the image of an older man:

Note   Programs like Adobe Photoshop and GIMP have a Healing Brush tool for removing blemishes and imperfections by calculating surrounding texture and tone, and then blending the sampled pixels in for a seamless repair. While Paint.NET does not offer a healing tool, the careful use of the Clone Stamp Tool can still yield excellent results.

---

1. Open the practice image *Ch6_Remove_Blemishes* in Paint.NET.

2. Duplicate the Background layer by clicking the Duplicate Layer tab at the bottom of the Layers Window—rename the layer *Blemish Repair* (or something similar).

3. Select the *Clone Stamp* Tool (L); set the *Brush width* to 10 and the hardness to 0—start at the top cloning out the blemishes (highlighted in Figure 6-19) and work downward, adjusting the brush size as needed.

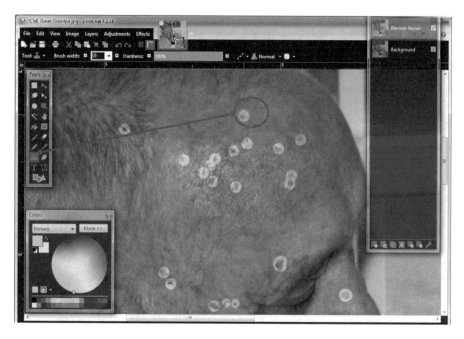

Figure 6-19. *Start cloning out the blemishes from the top and work downward*

4. Continue working downward, adjusting the brush size as needed; leave the largest blemishes for now (Figure 6-20).

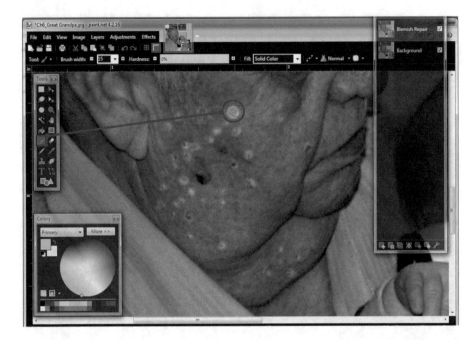

Figure 6-20. *Continue working downward, leaving the largest blemishes*

5. We'll finish up by working on the largest blemishes (Figure 6-21) —the smaller blemishes were done first to provide enough good image area to sample from.

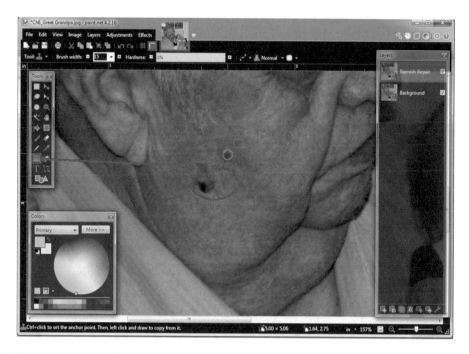

Figure 6-21. *The largest blemishes will be removed last*

We can now see the result, which looks much better in Figure 6-22.

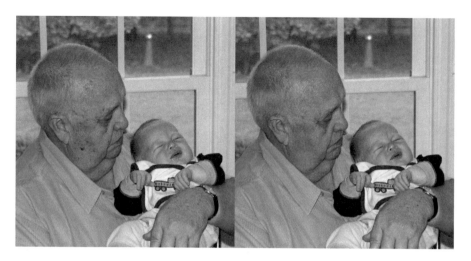

Figure 6-22. *The before and after comparison*

TUTORIAL 18: REPAIRING SCRATCHES AND DAMAGE

We'll wrap this chapter up by repairing a photograph that has been damaged
by scratches and has some areas of "dust" to clean up:

1. Open the practice image *Ch6_Scratched_Photo* in Paint.NET.

2. Duplicate the Background layer by clicking the Duplicate Layer
   tab at the bottom of the Layers Window—rename the layer
   Dust and Scratch Repair (or something similar).

3. We'll first attack some of the dust; using the *Lasso Tool* (S,S),
   draw several selections around the dust in the upper-left area
   of the image as shown in Figure 6-23 (make sure the *Add
   (Union)* selection mode is active).

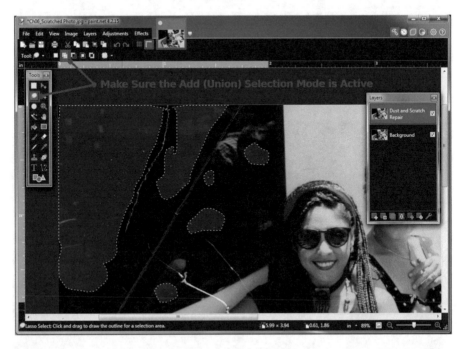

Figure 6-23. *Using the Lasso Tool, draw selections around the areas
of dust as shown*

4. Open the *Median* dialog (Effects ➤ Noise ➤ Median).

5. Move the Radius slider to 2, then click OK; this is just enough
    to obliterate the dust specks and maintain detail as shown in
    Figure 6-24. Examine the rest of the image and repeat this step
    as needed.

Figure 6-24. *Set the Radius to 2 in the Median dialog*

6. Deactivate the selections (Ctrl+D).

7. Select the *Clone Stamp* Tool (L); set the *Brush width* to 10 and
    the hardness to 50%—start at the top cloning out the tear
    (highlighted in Figure 6-25) and work downward, adjusting the
    brush size as needed.

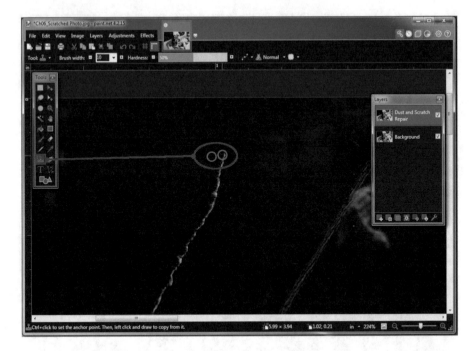

Figure 6-25. *Use the Clone Stamp Tool to remove the tear shown*

8. Lower the brush size to 5 pixels and remove tears shown
    (Figure 6-26).

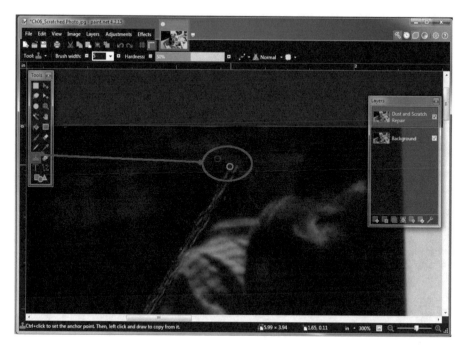

Figure 6-26. *Use the Clone Stamp Tool to remove the tear shown*

9. Continue working downward and toward the right, adjusting the
brush size as needed (Figure 6-27).

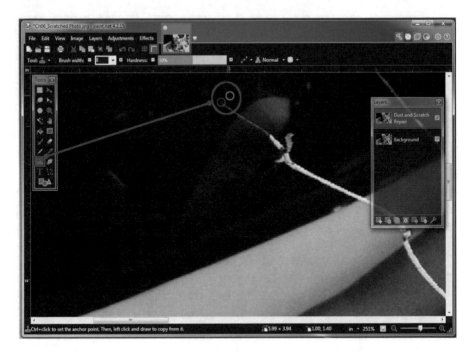

Figure 6-27. *Continue working down and across, adjusting the brush size as needed*

10. After the left portion of the image is complete, work on the last of the damage on the right as shown in Figure 6-28.

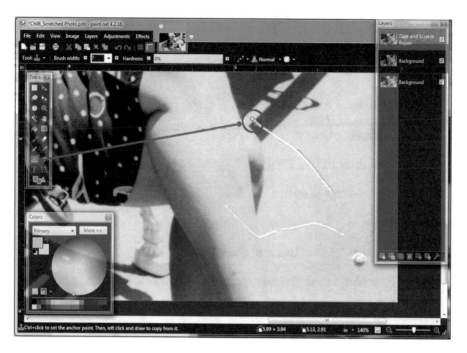

Figure 6-28. *Finish repairing the last of the damage on the right side of the image*

Review the image closely to clean up any overlooked areas. Figure 6-29 shows the before and after comparison, which demonstrates how useful Paint.NET can be for repairing and restoring damaged photographs.

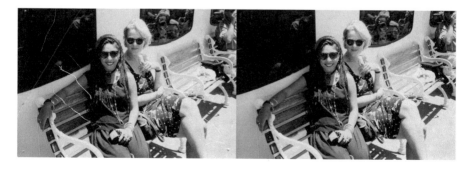

Figure 6-29. *The before and after comparison*

Chapter Conclusion

We're now more than halfway through the lessons, and you've learned a lot so far!

Here's a recap of what was covered:

- Removing Unwanted Objects

- Straightening an Image

- Brightening Teeth

- Removing Blemishes

- Repairing Scratches and Damage

In the next chapter, we'll learn some basic lessons about compositing images.

CHAPTER 7

Compositing Images

In this chapter, we'll cover the basics of adding elements to an image (in the upcoming tutorial, we'll be adding birds in flight to an image) as well as replacing backgrounds.

The tutorials covered in this chapter are

- Tutorial 19: Adding Elements to an Image

- Tutorial 20: Simple Background Replacement

- Chapter Conclusion

TUTORIAL 19: ADDING ELEMENTS TO AN IMAGE

In this tutorial, we're going to add a flock of birds in flight to the image of the street lamp we worked with in the previous chapter. While most would agree that it looks much better without the distracting power lines, it would probably be a more interesting image with other visual elements in it.

1. Open the practice image *Ch7_Composite_Lamp*.

2. Duplicate the Background layer by clicking the Duplicate Layer tab at the bottom of the Layers Window and rename it *Birds Added*, or something similar.

3. Open the second practice image Ch7_Flying_Birds.

4. Select the entire image (of the birds in flight) (Edit ➤ Select All).

5. Copy the image (Edit ➤ Copy).

© Phillip Whitt 2022
P. Whitt, *Practical Paint.NET*, https://doi.org/10.1007/978-1-4842-7283-1_7

6. Click the thumbnail tab of the first practice image in the *Image List* (Figure 7-1) to make it active.

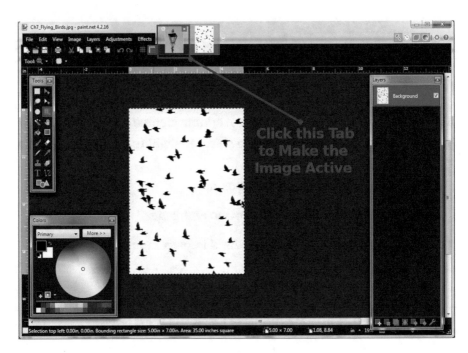

Figure 7-1. *Click the thumbnail tab shown to make the image active*

7. Paste the copied image of the birds over the image of the lamp (Edit ➤ Paste into New Layer).

8. Double-click the duplicate layer's preview thumbnail to launch the *Layer Properties* dialog; rename the layer *Birds* or something similar. Change the blend mode to *Multiply* (which essentially blends away the white pixels), then click OK (Figure 7-2).

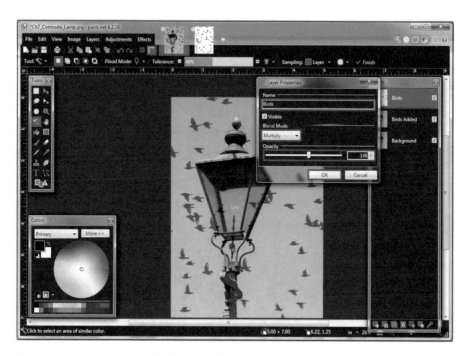

Figure 7-2. *Rename the layer, then change the blend mode to Multiply, lower the opacity to about 146, then click OK*

9. Using the *Eraser Tool* with a brush size of 8–10 pixels and a hardness of 0, remove the portions of the birds that would be blocked by the lamp head when viewing (Figure 7-3); be careful not to erase too much so there won't be a noticeable gap— zoom in as close as necessary.

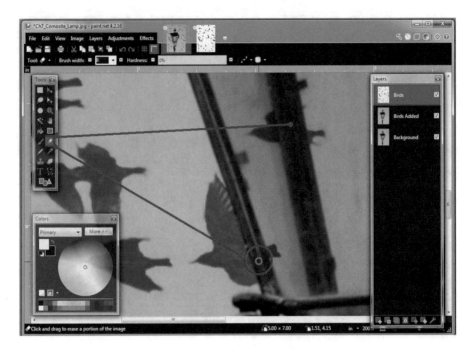

Figure 7-3. *Using the Eraser Tool, remove the portions that would be blocked by the lamp*

10. Examine the lamp head and repeat the process as necessary; zoom in as needed (Figure 7-4).

Figure 7-4. *Continue the process as needed around the lamp head*

11.   Move downward and repeat the process below the lamp head
      as shown in Figure 7-5.

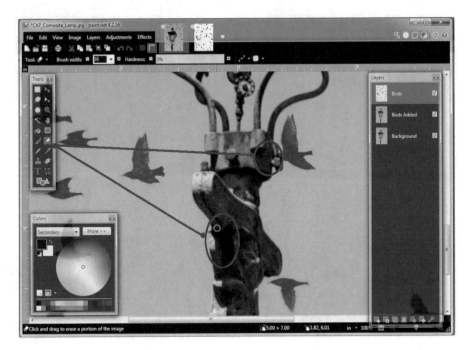

Figure 7-5. *Continue the process as needed below the lamp head*

12. After the erasing has been completed, double-click the layer's preview thumbnail to launch the *Layer Properties* dialog and increase the opacity to 255.

13. Open the *Gaussian Blur* dialog (Effects ➤ Blurs ➤ Gaussian Blur) and move the *Radius* slider until the numeric readout is 2, then click OK (Figure 7-6).

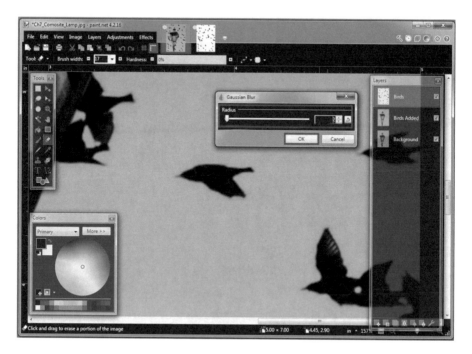

Figure 7-6. *Move the radius slider until the numeric readout is 2*

14. Click the duplicate background layer (this is the layer that was named *Birds Added*).

15. Using the *Lasso Select Tool* (S,S), draw selections around the birds showing through the glass as shown in Figure 7-7 (make sure the *Add (Union)* selection mode is active).

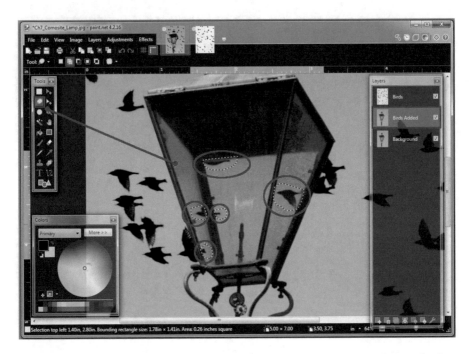

Figure 7-7. *Make a selection around each bird showing through the glass panes*

16.   Copy the selected areas (Edit ➤ Copy), then paste into a new layer (Edit ➤ Paste into New Layer).

17.   Deactivate the selections (Edit ➤ Deselect).

18.   Double-click the new layer's preview thumbnail to launch the *Layer Properties* dialog; rename the layer *Glass Panes* or something similar.

19.   Move the layer to the top of the layer stack (Layers ➤ Move Layer to Top).

20. Double-click the duplicate layer's preview thumbnail to launch the *Layer Properties* dialog; lower the layer opacity to about 95 as shown in Figure 7-8—because the glass panes have a hazy coating of pollen and dirt, the birds' visibility is obscured just enough to make the composite appear more realistic.

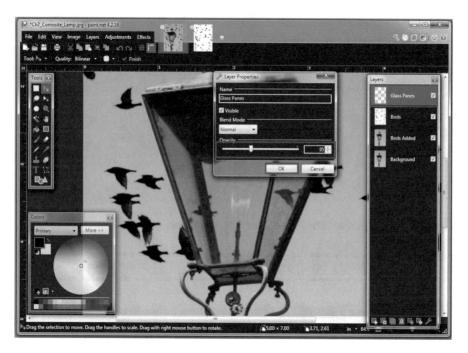

Figure 7-8. *Lower the layer's opacity to make the birds appear as though being viewed through the glass with a hazy coating*

The image now has a little more visual interest, as seen in Figure 7-9. When done, save the work as a pdn file (Paint.NET's native file format) or close it out.

Figure 7-9. *The before and after comparison*

TUTORIAL 20: SIMPLE BACKGROUND REPLACEMENT

In this lesson, we'll essentially extract the subject from one photo and place it against another that will serve as a scenic background:

1. Open the practice images *Ch7_Waterfall_Background* and *Ch7_Background_Change* (this is the same image we used in one of the tutorials in the last chapter, but with a different title) in Paint.NET.

2. Using the *Magic Wand Tool* (S,S,S,S) with the *Flood Mode* set to *Contiguous* and the *Tolerance* set to 42%, click in the area shown in Figure 7-10; the result you get should resemble this closely.

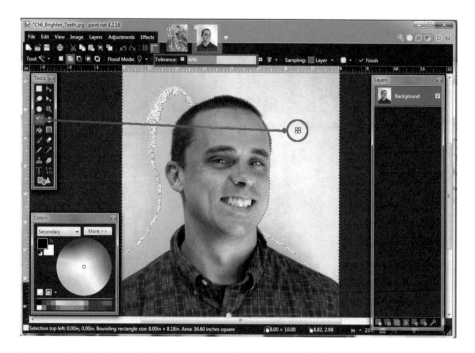

Figure 7-10. *Use the Magic Wand Tool and click in the area shown*

3. Remove the selected areas by cutting the pixels (Edit ➤ Cut).

4. Repeat Steps 2 and 3 in the area shown in Figure 7-11.

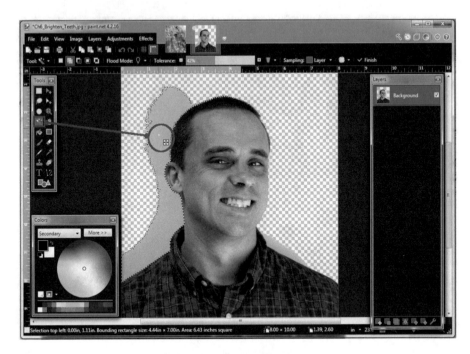

Figure 7-11. *Select and cut the pixels shown*

5. Using the *Eraser Tool* (E) with the brush hardness set to 50%, remove any remaining background pixels; zoom in and adjust the brush size as needed (Figure 7-12).

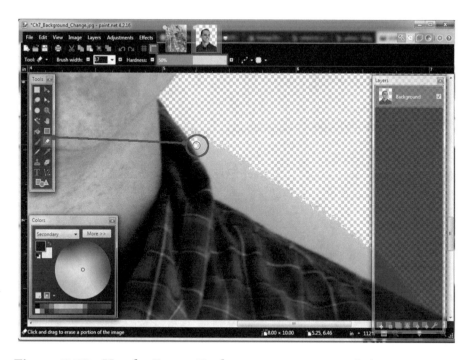

Figure 7-12. *Use the Eraser Tool to remove any remaining background pixels*

6. Set the brush hardness to zero and work along the hair to remove the fringe as shown in Figure 7-13; adjust the brush size and zoom in as needed.

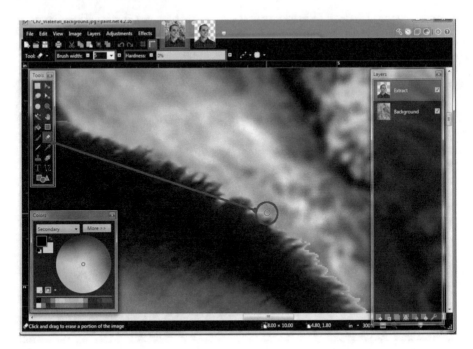

Figure 7-13. *Use the Eraser Tool to remove the fringe along the edge of the hair*

7. Set the Eraser Tool's brush hardness to 50%.

8. Zoom in along the face and smooth out any jagged edges as shown in Figure 7-14; zoom in and adjust the brush size as needed.

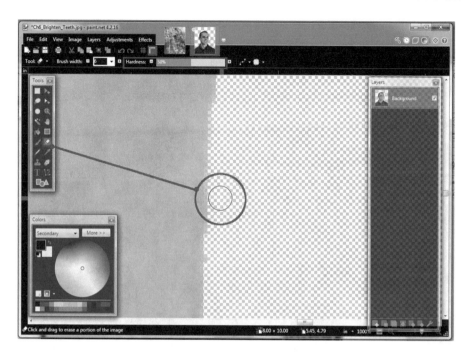

Figure 7-14. *Use the Eraser Tool to smooth out any jagged areas along the face*

9. Check around the image for any stray pixels, and remove them as needed.

10. Now we'll get ready to place the extracted subject over the new background—follow these steps in the order shown:

    1. Select the subject (Edit ➤ Select All).

    2. Copy the selected image (Edit ➤ Copy).

    3. Click the thumbnail of *Ch7_Waterfall_Background* in the *Image List* to make it the active image.

    4. Paste the extracted image into a new layer over the new background (Edit ➤ Paste into New Layer).

225

11.   Double-click the new layer's preview thumbnail to launch the *Layer Properties* dialog; rename the layer *Extracted Subject* or something similar.

12.   The result should closely resemble the one shown in Figure 7-15.

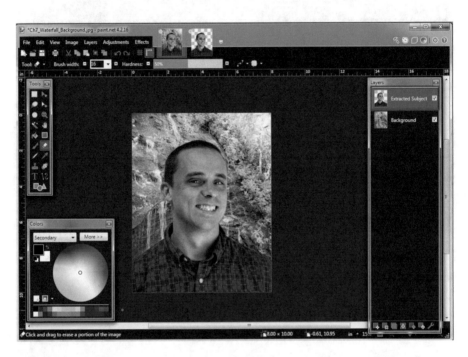

Figure 7-15. *The result should closely resemble the one shown here*

13.   Click the Background layer's thumbnail preview to make it active.

14.   The new background is a bit too sharp, so we'll blur it a bit to create a mild depth-of-field effect to put more emphasis on the man; open the *Gaussian Blur* dialog (Effects ➤ Blurs ➤ Gaussian Blur) and move the *Radius* slider until the numeric readout is 5, then click OK (Figure 7-16).

Figure 7-16. *Blur the background slightly to place more emphasis on the subject*

By replacing the plain background in the original (which was just a wall), we now have a more interesting photo (Figure 7-17). When done, save the work as a pdn file (Paint.NET's native file format) or close it out.

Figure 7-17. *The before and after comparison*

Chapter Conclusion

Composites can get complex and involved (and for some projects, Photoshop and GIMP are better suited). For basic projects such as the ones covered in this chapter, Paint.NET is a capable program.

Here's a recap of what was covered:

- Adding birds to an image

- Replacing a background

In the next chapter, we'll learn some drawing basics using Paint.NET.

CHAPTER 8

Drawing Basics

In this chapter, we'll cover some drawing basics using Paint.NET. The primary purpose of this chapter is to better acquaint the reader with some of the drawing tools. For those with experience in creating art (either conventionally or digitally), then these lessons should be easy.

The tutorials covered in this chapter are

- Using the Pencil and Brush Tools

- Tutorial 21: Drawing a Simple Sketch

- Tutorial 22: Drawing a Heart on a Textured Background

- Tutorial 23: Drawing a Smart Phone

- Chapter Conclusion

Note   Paint.NET is only capable of creating or editing *raster (or bitmapped)* images. Raster graphics are pixel-based and not scalable without causing the image quality to degrade. *Vector* images (such as the type created in the open source program Inkscape) are scalable, which means they can be scaled without loss of quality.

© Phillip Whitt 2022
P. Whitt, *Practical Paint.NET*, https://doi.org/10.1007/978-1-4842-7283-1_8

Using the Pencil and Brush Tools

The default drawing and painting tools are rather rudimentary; the *Pencil Tool* stroke is only 1 pixel wide with no option for adjusting the size or hardness. The only options available for this tool are changing the stroke color and blend mode; a few examples are shown in Figure 8-1.

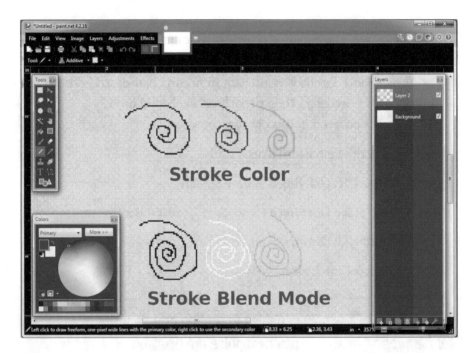

Figure 8-1. *The Pencil Tool's stroke color and blend mode can be changed*

There are more options available for the Paintbrush Tool. As we can see in Figure 8-2, the *Antialiasing* can be disabled or enabled, and the *Brush width* and *hardness* can be changed, as well as the *Blend Modes*.

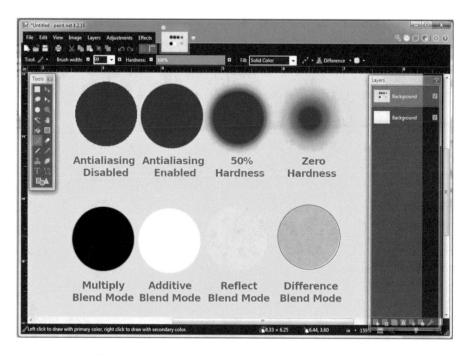

Figure 8-2. *The Pencil Tool's Antialias can be disabled/enabled, and the Brush width, hardness, and Blend Mode can be changed*

Note   Brush Factory V 2.0 is a plugin for Paint.NET that offers a variety of dynamic brushes with customizable shapes. Brush Factory V 2.0 is discussed in more detail in the Appendix of this book.

TUTORIAL 21: DRAWING A SIMPLE SKETCH

In this tutorial, we're going to create a simple sketch using Paint.NET:

1. Open the practice image *Ch8_Flower_To_Outline* (we'll be tracing over this image to create the sketch).

2. Add a new layer (Layers ➤ Add New Layer).

3. Double-click the new layer's preview thumbnail to launch the Layer Properties dialog; rename the layer Outline or something similar, then click OK.

4. In the *Colors Window*, change the *Primary Color* to black.

5. Using the *Paintbrush Tool* (B) with the brush width set to 8 and the hardness set to 100%, trace around the outer edge of the flower as shown Figure 8-3.

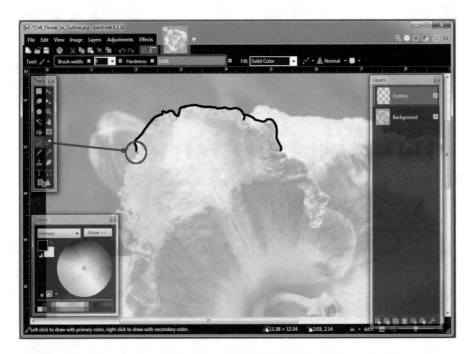

Figure 8-3. *Trace around the outer edge of the image*

6. When the outer edge is completed, it should resemble the example shown in Figure 8-4.

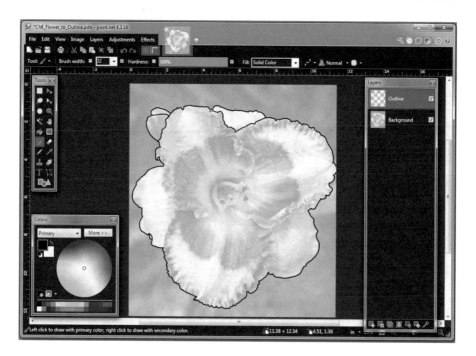

Figure 8-4. *The outer edge traced*

7. Trace around the edge of the dark inner portion of the flower as shown in Figure 8-5.

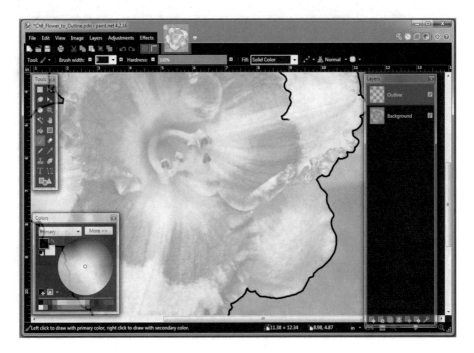

Figure 8-5. *Trace around the outer edge of the dark inner portion of the flower*

8.   Continue tracing; for thinner lines, reduce the brush width to about 5 pixels (Figure 8-6).

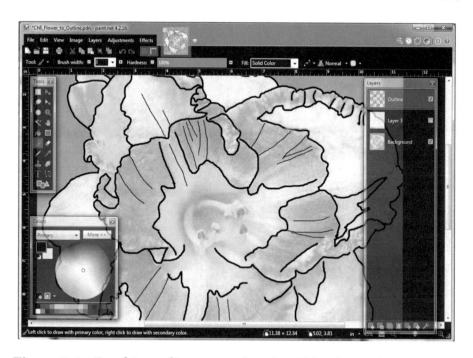

Figure 8-6. *For thinner lines, use a brush width of 5 pixels*

9.   When finished, your result should resemble the example shown
     in Figure 8-7.

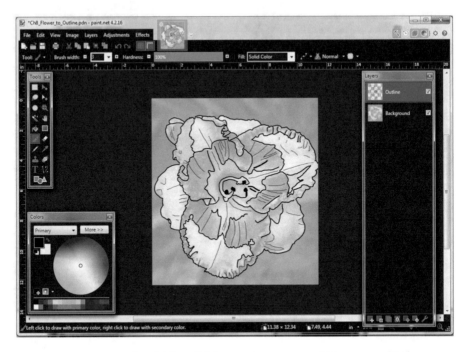

Figure 8-7. *Your result should bear some resemblance to this example*

10. Click the Background layer to make it active.

11. Add a new layer (Layers ➤ Add New Layer)—this will add it between the Background and Outline layers.

12. Double-click the new layer's preview thumbnail to launch the Layer Properties dialog; rename the layer *White Background* or something similar, then click OK.

13. In the *Colors Window*, change the *Primary Color* to white.

14. Using the *Rectangle Select Tool*, draw a selection around the new layer.

15. Fill the selection with white (Edit ➤ Fill Selection).

The final result should look something like the example in Figure 8-8—it won't be exactly as shown, of course, but that's okay. The main objective is to acquaint new users with the drawing tools in Paint.NET. When done, save the work as a pdn file (Paint.NET's native file format) or close it out.

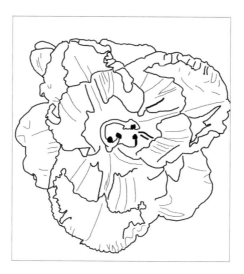

Figure 8-8. *The final result*

TUTORIAL 22: DRAWING A HEART ON A TEXTURED BACKGROUND

In this lesson, we'll use the *Shapes Tool* to draw a heart on a textured background (it will be stylized a bit). This lesson will help ease the beginner into creating graphics:

1. Open the practice image *Ch8_Texture* in Paint.NET.

2. Add a new layer by clicking the *Add New Layer* tab at the bottom of the Layers Window.

3. Double-click the new layer's preview thumbnail to launch the Layer Properties dialog; rename the layer *Heart* or something similar, then change the *Blend Mode* to *Color Burn*, and click OK (Figure 8-9).

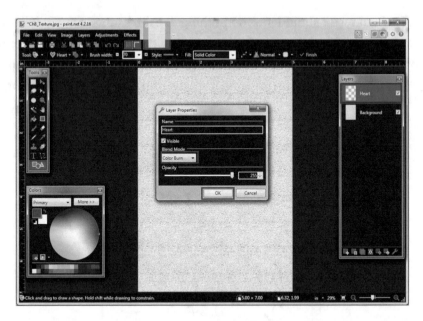

Figure 8-9. *Rename the new layer and change the Blend Mode to Color Burn as shown*

4. Change the *Primary Color* to red; in the *RGB* setting, set the value in the red slider to 255 and to 0 in the green and blue sliders (Figure 8-10).

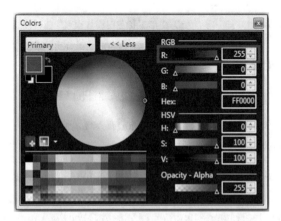

Figure 8-10. *Set the Primary Color to red as shown.*

5.   Click the *Shapes Tool* (O,O), and select the heart shape from the drop-down menu; make sure the *Draw Filled Shape* mode is selected (Figure 8-11).

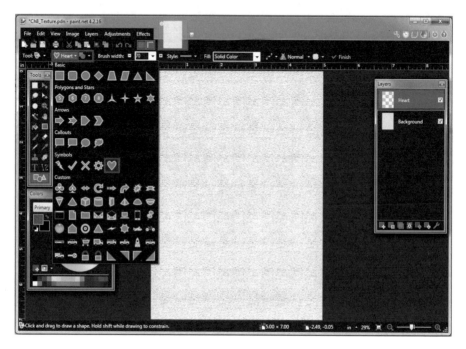

Figure 8-11. *Select the heart shape with the Draw Filled Shape mode selected*

6. Click and drag to draw a heart resembling the example in Figure 8-12.

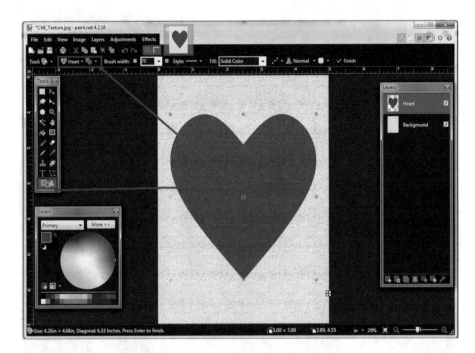

Figure 8-12. *Draw a heart shape like the one shown*

7. Add a new layer by clicking the *Add New Layer* tab at the bottom of the Layers Window.

8. Double-click the new layer's preview thumbnail to launch the *Layer Properties* dialog; rename the layer *Cutout* or something similar, then click OK.

9. Change the *Primary Color* to white.

10. Click the *Shapes Tool* (O,O), and select the heart shape from the drop-down menu; make sure the *Draw Filled Shape* mode is selected.

11. Click and drag to draw a heart a little off-center left (on the new layer named *Cutout*) resembling the example in Figure 8-13; this will be used as a means to remove a portion of the main heart graphic.

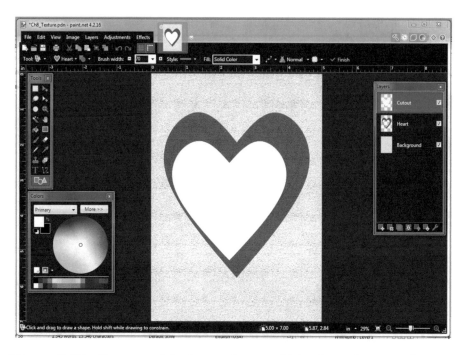

Figure 8-13. *Draw a white heart shape within the red one as shown*

12. Using the *Magic Wand Tool* (S,S,S,S), click inside the white heart shape to select it.

13. Make the layer named *Heart* by clicking the layer's preview thumbnail in the *Layers Window*; the inner part of the red heart shape is now selected.

14. Hide the visibility of the layer named *Cutout* by ticking the checkbox on the layer preview thumbnail.

15. Erase the pixels (Edit ➤ Erase Selection)—the inner part of the red heart has been removed (Figure 8-14).

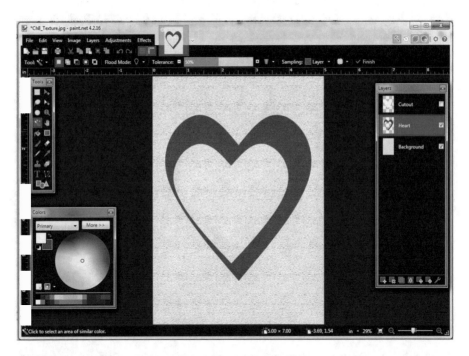

Figure 8-14. *The inner part of the heart has now been removed, creating a stylized graphic*

The final result should look something like the example in Figure 8-15—it may not be exactly as shown, of course, but that's okay. The main objective is to acquaint new users with the Shapes Tools in Paint.NET. When done, save the work as a pdn file (Paint.NET's native file format) or close it out.

Figure 8-15. *The final result*

TUTORIAL 23: DRAWING A SMART PHONE (BOLTBAIT'S PLUGIN PACK REQUIRED)

In this lesson, we'll add some detail to a basic smart phone shape. The BoltBait Plugin Pack will need to be installed to do this tutorial:

1. Open the New dialog (File ➤ New); set the width to 1500 pixels, the height to 2100 pixels, and the resolution to 300 pixels/inch, then click OK (Figure 8-16).

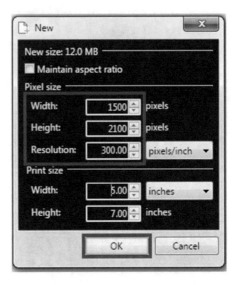

Figure 8-16. *Set the width to 1500 pixels, the height to 2100 pixels, and the resolution to 300 pixels/inch, then click OK*

2. Add a new layer by clicking the *Add New Layer* tab at the bottom of the Layers Window.

3. Double-click the new layer's preview thumbnail to launch the Layer Properties dialog; rename the layer *Phone Body* or something similar, then click OK.

4. Change the *Primary Color* to black.

5. Click the *Shapes Tool* (with the *Draw/Fill* mode selected), and select the *Smart Phone* shape (Figure 8-17).

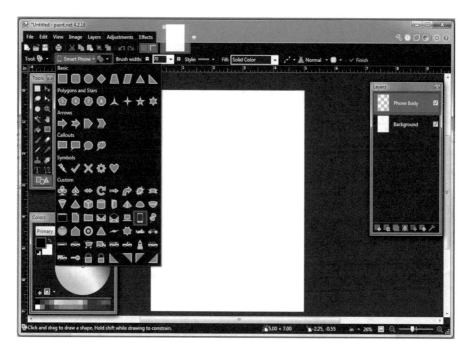

Figure 8-17. *Select the Smart Phone shape with the Draw Filled Shape mode selected*

6. Click and drag to draw the phone (approximately 2 inches x 4 inches) using the rulers as a guide as shown in Figure 8-18; click and drag the graphic to the approximate center of the document.

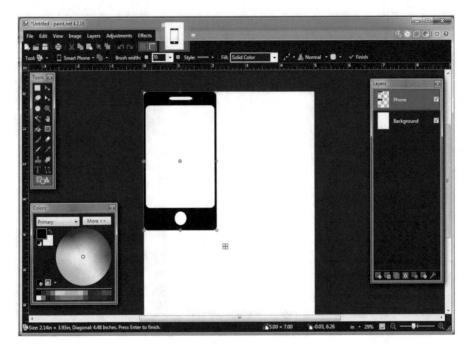

Figure 8-18. *Draw the phone body about 2 inches x 4 inches, then move to the center of the document*

7. Add a new layer by clicking the *Add New Layer* tab at the bottom of the Layers Window.

8. Double-click the new layer's preview thumbnail to launch the Layer Properties dialog; rename the layer *Screen* or something similar, then click OK.

9. Using the Magic Wand Tool (S,S,S,S), click inside the phone's screen area; make sure under *Sampling*, the *Image* setting is selected (Figure 8-19).

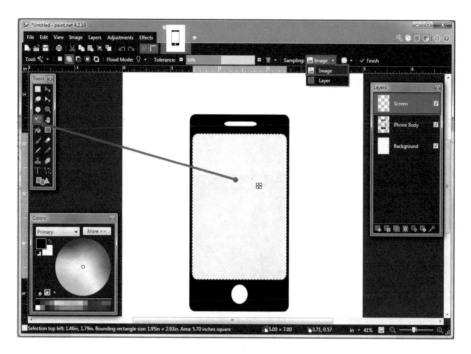

Figure 8-19. *Using the Magic Wand Tool, click inside the area shown to select it; make sure the Image Sampling Mode is selected*

10. In the *Colors Window*, change the *Primary Color* using these values in the *RGB* settings:

- R-0

- G-255

- B-255

11. Change the *Secondary Color* using these values in the *RGB* settings:

- R-254

- G-0

- B-222

12.   Using the *Gradient Tool*, click and drag from top to bottom within the selection as shown in Figure 8-20.

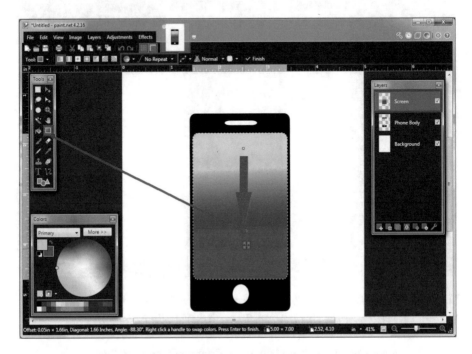

Figure 8-20. *Draw a gradient within the selection as shown*

13.   Deactivate the selection (Edit ➤ Deselect).

14.   Add a new layer by clicking the *Add New Layer* tab at the bottom of the Layers Window.

15.   Double-click the new layer's preview thumbnail to launch the Layer Properties dialog; rename the layer *Earpiece/Mouthpiece* or something similar, then click OK.

16.   Change the *Primary Color* to gray (the red, green, and blue values all being set to 128)—set the *Secondary Color* to black.

17. Using the *Paint Bucket Tool* (F) with the *Fill Mode* set to *Percent 50* and the *Sampling Mode* set to *Image*, click inside the earpiece and mouthpiece to fill with the pattern as shown in Figure 8-21.

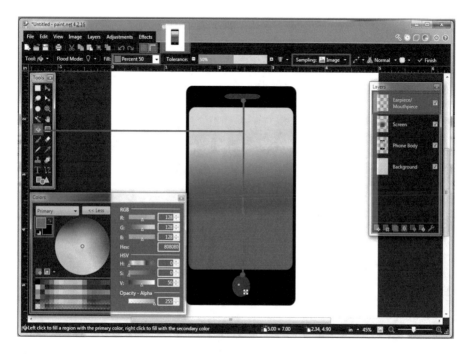

Figure 8-21. *Using the Paint Bucket Tool, fill the areas shown*

18. Add a new layer (Layers ➤ Add New Layer).

19. Double-click the new layer's preview thumbnail to launch the Layer Properties dialog; rename the layer *Charge Icon* or something similar, then click OK.

20. In the *Colors Window*, change the *Primary Color* to yellow using these values in the *RGB* settings:

- R-255

- G-255

- B-0

21. Click the Shapes Tool (with the *Draw/Fill* mode selected), and select the *Zot* shape (Figure 8-22).

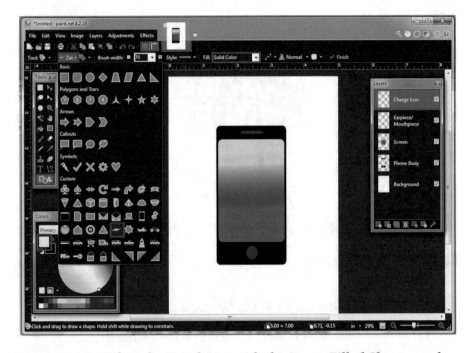

Figure 8-22. *Select the Zot shape with the Draw Filled Shape mode selected*

22. Click and drag from left to right to apply the graphic as shown in Figure 8-23.

Figure 8-23. *Click and drag from left to right to apply the graphic*

23. Now, we'll add a shine along the top of the phone to finish things off; add a new layer (Layers ➤ Add New Layer).

24. Double-click the new layer's preview thumbnail to launch the Layer Properties dialog; rename the layer Shine or something similar, then click OK.

25. In the *Colors Window*, change the *Primary Color* to white.

26. Using the *Rectangle Select Tool*, draw a narrow rectangle along the top of the phone as shown in Figure 8-24.

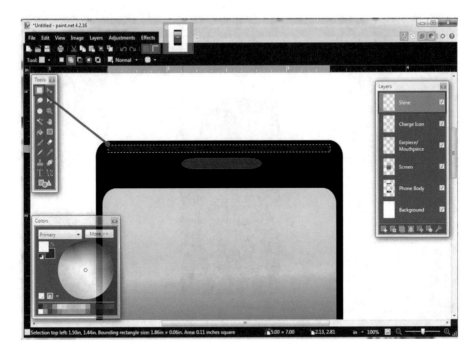

Figure 8-24. *Draw a narrow rectangle as shown*

27. Using the *Paint Bucket Tool* (F), click in the selection to fill it with white.

28. Deactivate the selection (Edit ➤ Deselect).

29. Open the *Gaussian Blur* dialog (Effects ➤ Blurs ➤ Gaussian Blur), and adjust the *Radius* to 10, then click OK (Figure 8-25).

Figure 8-25. *Adjust the Radius to 10, then click OK*

The final result should look something like the example in Figure 8-26—it may not be exactly as shown, but should be pretty close. The main objective is to acquaint new users with the Shapes Tools in Paint.NET. When done, save the work as a pdn file (Paint.NET's native file format) or close it out.

Figure 8-26. *The final result*

Note   In this chapter, you created art by working with already existing graphical elements (such as tracing the flower to create a sketch) or predesigned shapes (such as the heart and the smart phone). In the next chapter, you'll create digital art from scratch.

Chapter Conclusion

We covered a lot in this chapter. As we can see, Paint.NET allows the user to create impressive graphics.

Here's a recap of what was covered:

- Using the Pencil and Brush Tools
- Drawing a Simple Sketch
- Drawing a Heart on a Textured Background
- Drawing a Smart Phone

In the next chapter, we'll create some more illustrations from scratch using Paint.NET.

CHAPTER 9

Creating Digital Artwork

In the previous chapter, we created a bit of digital art by using already existing elements and adding to (and incorporating) predesigned shapes. In this chapter, all of the art in the upcoming tutorials will be a bit more involved.

The tutorials covered in this chapter are

- Tutorial 24: Creating a Scenic Sunset

- Tutorial 25: Drawing a Shamrock

- Tutorial 26: Drawing a Ladybug

- Chapter Conclusion

TUTORIAL 24: CREATING A SCENIC SUNSET

In this lesson, we'll use Paint.NET to create a digital illustration of a sunset behind a mountain range:

1. Open the New dialog (File ➤ New); set the width to 3000 pixels, the height to 2400 pixels, and the resolution to 300 pixels/inch, then click OK (Figure 9-1).

© Phillip Whitt 2022
P. Whitt, *Practical Paint.NET*, https://doi.org/10.1007/978-1-4842-7283-1_9

Figure 9-1. *Set the width to 3000 pixels, the height to 2400 pixels, and the resolution to 300 pixels/inch, then click OK*

2. Add a new layer (Layers ➤ Add New Layer).

3. Double-click the new layer's preview thumbnail to launch the Layer Properties dialog; rename the layer *Sunset Gradient*, or something similar, then click OK.

4. In the *Colors Window*, change the *Primary Color* using these values in the *RGB* settings:

   - R-255

   - G-67

   - B-0

5. In the *Colors Window*, change the *Secondary Color* using these values in the RGB settings:

   - R-255

   - G-106

   - B-0

6. Use the *Gradient Tool* (G) to click and drag from top to bottom the as shown in Figure 9-2.

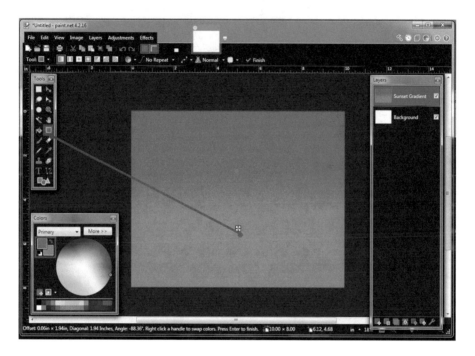

Figure 9-2. *Draw a gradient from top to bottom as shown*

7. Add a new layer (Layers ➤ Add New Layer).

8. Double-click the new layer's preview thumbnail to launch the Layer Properties dialog; rename the layer *Sun*, or something similar, then click OK.

9. Click the *Shapes Tool* (with the *Draw/Fill* mode selected), and select the *Ellipse* shape (Figure 9-3).

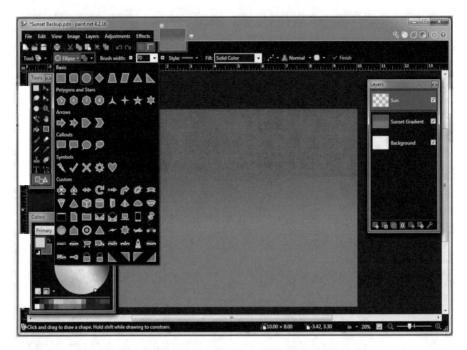

Figure 9-3. *Select the Ellipse shape with the Draw Filled Shape mode selected*

10. Draw a circle (hold the Shift key) approximately 2 inches in diameter as shown in Figure 9-4.

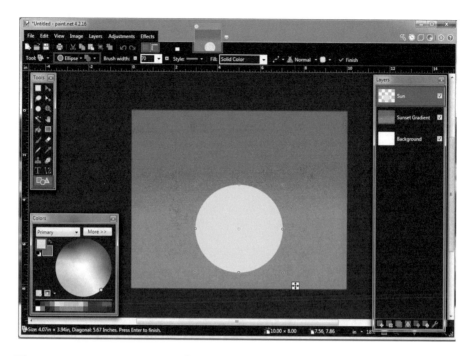

Figure 9-4. *Draw a circle (hold the Shift key) about 2 inches in diameter as shown*

11. Open the Gaussian Blur dialog (Effects ➤ Blurs ➤ Gaussian Blur), and adjust the Radius to 60, then click OK (Figure 9-5).

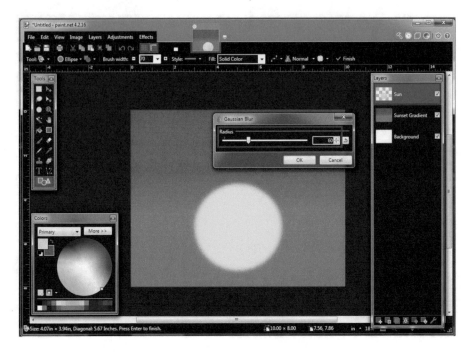

Figure 9-5. *Adjust the Radius to 60, then click OK*

12. Add a new layer (Layers ➤ Add New Layer).

13. Double-click the new layer's preview thumbnail to launch
     the Layer Properties dialog; rename the layer *Mountains-
     Background*, or something similar, then click OK.

14. In the *Colors Window*, change the *Primary Color* using these
     values in the RGB settings:

     • R-135

     • G-106

     • B-255

15. Using the *Lasso Select Tool* (S,S), make an irregular selection
     similar to the one shown in Figure 9-6.

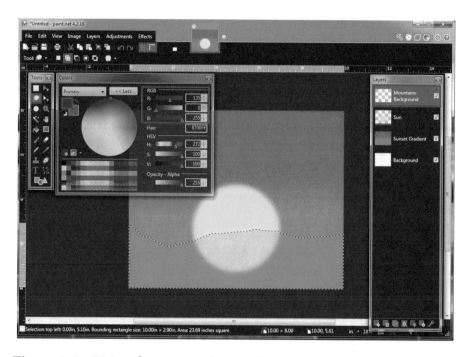

Figure 9-6. *Using the Lasso Select Tool, make an irregular selection similar to the one shown*

16. Using the *Paint Bucket Tool* (F), click in the selection to fill it with the purple hue.

17. Repeat Steps 12–15 using these variations:

- Name the new layer *Mountains-Middleground* (or something similar).

- In the *Colors Window*, change the *Primary Color* to a darker purple hue by adjusting the red slider to 63 and the blue slider to 119.

- Using the Lasso Select Tool (S,S), make an irregular selection.

- Using the Paint Bucket Tool (F), click in the selection to fill it with the darker purple hue (Figure 9-7)—we can see the mountains now being formed.

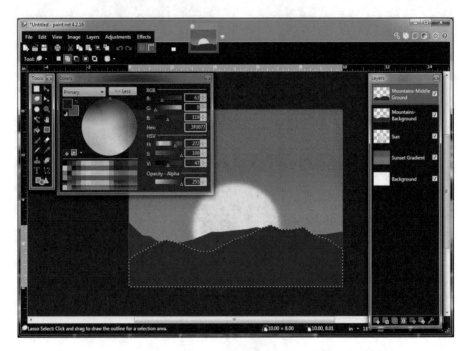

Figure 9-7. *The mountains being formed*

18.   Once more, repeat Steps 12–15 using these variations:

- Name the new layer *Mountains-Foreground* (or something similar).

- In the *Colors Window*, change the *Primary Color to a very dark* purple hue by adjusting the red slider to 32 and the blue slider to 61.

- Using the *Lasso Select Tool* (S,S), make an irregular selection.

- Using the Paint Bucket Tool (F), click in the selection to fill it with the darkest purple hue (Figure 9-8)—we can see the last of the mountains being formed.

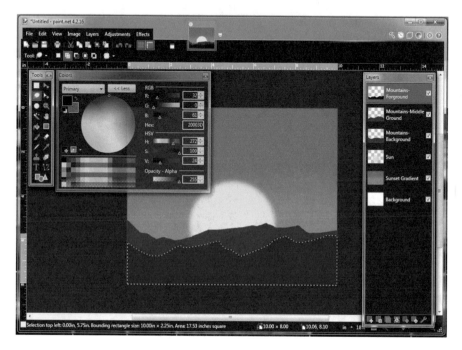

Figure 9-8. *The last of the mountains being formed*

19. Add a new layer (Layers ➤ Add New Layer).

20. Double-click the new layer's preview thumbnail to launch the Layer Properties dialog; rename the layer *Clouds*, or something similar, change the blend mode to *Multiply*, then click OK.

21. Using the *Lasso Select Tool* (S,S), draw several areas similar to those shown in Figure 9-9 (make sure the *Add (Union)* mode is selected).

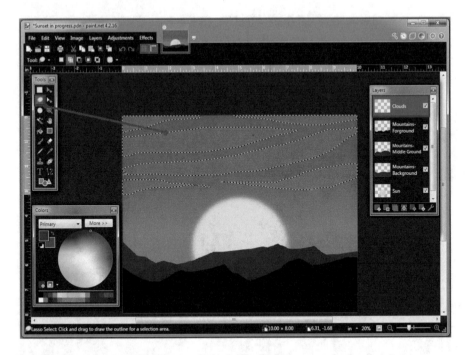

Figure 9-9. *Using the Lasso Select Tool, draw several selections similar to those shown*

22. In the *Colors Window*, change the *Primary Color* using these values in the RGB settings:

    - R-178

    - G-0

    - B-255

23. Fill the selected areas with the Primary Color (Edit ➤ Fill Selection).

24. Deactivate the selection (Edit ➤ Deselect).

25. Open the Gaussian Blur dialog (Effects ➤ Blurs ➤ Gaussian Blur), and adjust the Radius to about 163, then click OK (Figure 9-10), creating a few wispy clouds.

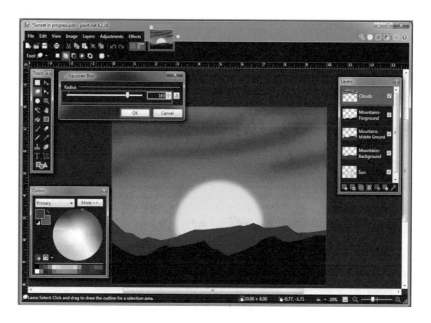

Figure 9-10. *Use the Gaussian Blur dialog to create a wispy cloud effect*

The final result should look something like the example in Figure 9-11. When done, save the work as a pdn file (Paint.NET's native file format) or close it out.

Figure 9-11. *The final result*

TUTORIAL 25: DRAWING A SHAMROCK

In this lesson, we'll use the *Shapes* and *Line Tools* to create a basic illustration of a shamrock:

1. Open the *New* dialog (File ➤ New); set the *width* and *height* to 1800 pixels and the resolution to 300 pixels/inch, then click OK (Figure 9-12).

Figure 9-12. *Set the width and height to 1800 pixels, the resolution to 300 pixels/inch, then click OK*

2. Double-click the background layer's preview thumbnail to launch the Layer Properties dialog; rename the layer *Sky* or something similar, then click OK.

3. In the *Colors Window*, change the *Primary Color* to a sky blue using these values (Figure 9-13):

    *   R-0

    *   G-145

    *   B-255

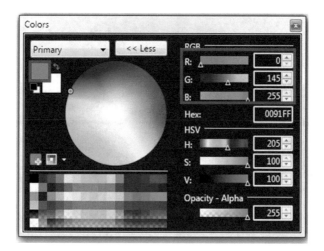

Figure 9-13. *Set red to 0, green to 145, and blue to 255*

4. Using the *Paint Bucket Tool* (F), click the image to fill with the sky blue color.

5. Add a new layer (Layers ➤ Add New Layer).

6. Double-click the new layer's preview thumbnail to launch the Layer Properties dialog; rename the layer *Shamrock Leaf* or something similar, then click OK.

7. Change the Primary Color to dark green using these values:

    •   R-38

    •   G-127

    •   B-0

8. Click the *Shapes Tool* (O,O), and select the heart shape from the drop-down menu; make sure the Draw Filled Shape mode is selected (Figure 9-14).

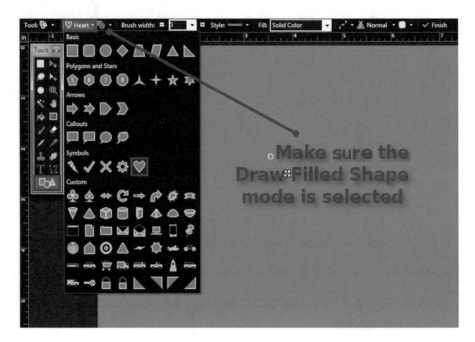

Figure 9-14. *Select the heart shape with the Draw Filled Shape mode selected*

9. Click and drag to draw a heart resembling the example in
    Figure 9-15.

Figure 9-15. *Draw a heart shape like the one shown; this will serve as a shamrock leaf*

10. Change the *Secondary Color* (Figure 9-16) to a light green using these numeric values:

- R-76

- G-255

- B-0

11. Using the *Magic Wand Tool* (S,S,S,S), click inside the heart shape to select it.

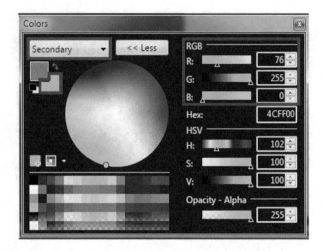

Figure 9-16. *Change the Secondary Color as shown*

12. Using the *Gradient Tool* (G) with the type set to *Linear (Reflected)* and *No Repeat*, draw a gradient in the selected area as shown in Figure 9-17.

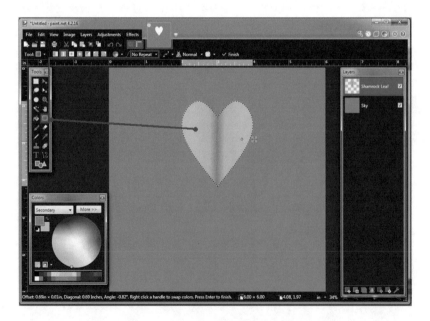

Figure 9-17. *Draw a gradient in the selected area as shown*

13. Deselect the shape (Edit ➤ Deselect).

14. Duplicate the layer named *Shamrock Leaf* (Layers ➤ Duplicate Layer).

15. We'll now rotate this layer; open the *Rotate/Zoom Tool* (Layers ➤ Rotate/Zoom)—move the top slider until the numeric value reads –125.00, then click OK (Figure 9-18).

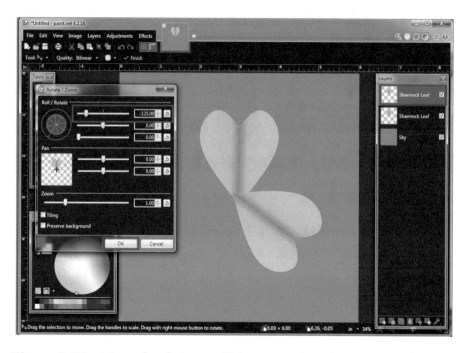

Figure 9-18. *Move the slider until the numeric value is –125, then click OK*

16. Duplicate the rotated layer (Layers ➤ Duplicate Layer).

17. Flip the duplicated layer horizontally (Layers ➤ Flip Horizontal) as shown in Figure 9-19.

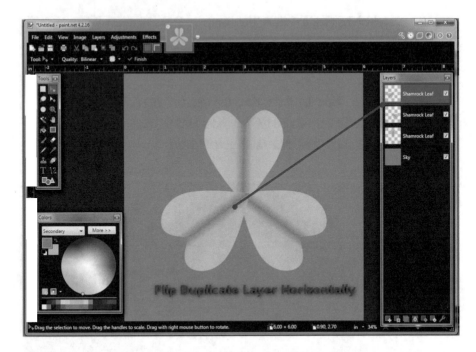

Figure 9-19. *Flip the duplicated layer horizontally*

18. Use the *Move Selected Pixels Tool* (M) to move the layers into
     place as shown in Figure 9-20.

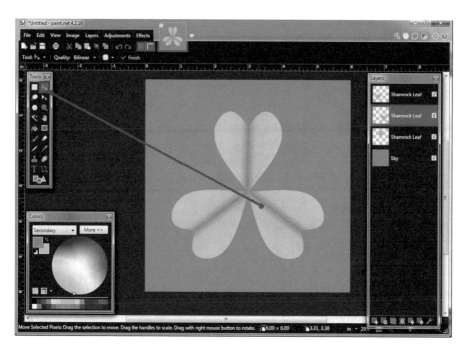

Figure 9-20. *Use the Move Selected Pixels Tool to move the layers into place as shown*

19. Add a new layer (Layers ➤ Add New Layer)—place it just above the background (Sky) layer.

20. Double-click the new layer's preview thumbnail to launch the Layer Properties dialog; rename the layer *Stem*, or something similar, then click OK.

21. Using the *Line/Curve Tool* (O) in the *Spline* mode, and the brush width set to 35 pixels, draw a line from the center of the shamrock down and bend slightly as shown in Figure 9-21.

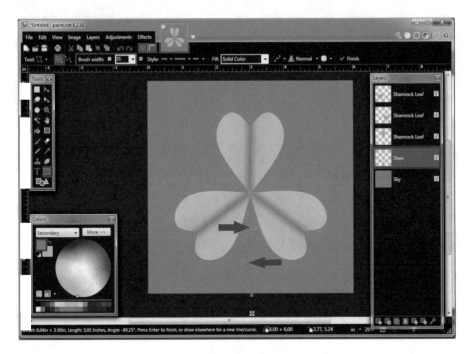

Figure 9-21. *Draw the stem using the Line/Curve Tool as shown*

The final result should look something like the example in Figure 9-22—it may not be exactly as shown, of course, but that's okay. When done, save the work as a pdn file (Paint.NET's native file format) or close it out.

Figure 9-22. *The final result*

TUTORIAL 26: DRAWING A LADYBUG

In this lesson, we'll draw a ladybug resting on the top leaf of the shamrock that was drawn in the previous tutorial (it's been provided as a practice image):

1. Open the practice image *Ch9_Shamrock_For_Ladybug.*

2. Add a new layer (Layers ➤ Add New Layer).

3. Double-click the new layer's preview thumbnail to launch the Layer Properties dialog; rename the layer *Body* or something similar, then click OK.

4. In the *Colors Window*, set the *Primary Color* to red.

5. Using the *Shapes Tool* (with the *Draw/Fill* mode selected), draw an ellipse and rotate it slightly as shown in Figure 9-23.

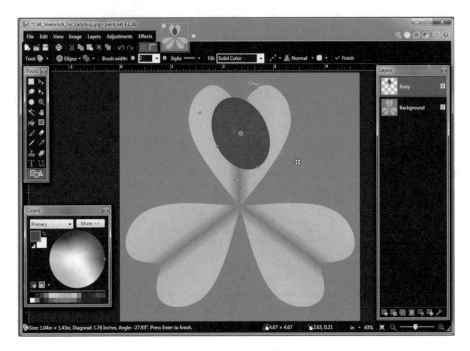

Figure 9-23. *Draw an ellipse and rotate it as shown*

6. Add a new layer (Layers ➤ Add New Layer).

7. In the *Colors Window*, set the *Primary Color* to black.

8. Double-click the new layer's preview thumbnail to launch the Layer Properties dialog; rename the layer Dividing Line or something similar, then click OK.

9. Using the *Line/Curve Tool* (set to *Bezier* mode and the *Brush width* to 5 pixels), draw a line bisecting the ellipse as shown in Figure 9-24—use the control nodes to form a slight arc.

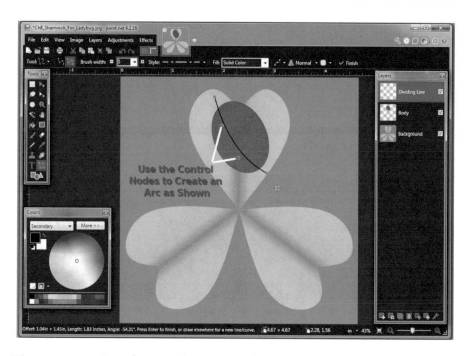

Figure 9-24. *Use the Line/Curve Tool to draw a line and the Control Nodes to form a slight arc as shown*

10. Now, we'll remove the excess portions of the line; click the layer's (named Body) preview thumbnail to make it active.

11. Using the *Magic Wand Tool (S,S,S,S)*, click inside the ellipse to select it.

12. Invert the selection (Edit ➤ Invert Selection).

13. Click the preview thumbnail of the layer named Dividing Line to make it *active*.

14. Erase the selection (Edit ➤ Erase Selection); this action will only remove the portions of the line outside of the ellipse (Figure 9-25).

277

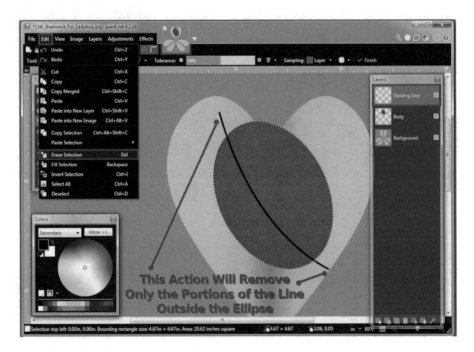

Figure 9-25. *Erase the selection to remove the excess parts of the line*

15. Add a new layer (Layers ➤ Add New Layer).

16. Double-click the new layer's preview thumbnail to launch the Layer Properties dialog; rename the layer *Spots* or something similar, then click OK.

17. Click the layer's (named *Body*) preview thumbnail to make it active.

18. Using the Magic Wand Tool, click the red ellipse to select the outline.

19. Click the preview window of the layer named Spots to make it *active*.

20.   Using the Paintbrush Tool (B) with the *Brush width* set to 80 and
the *hardness* set to 100%, click on several areas as shown in
Figure 9-26 to add some spots to the body (the selection will
keep the spots from extending beyond the ellipse).

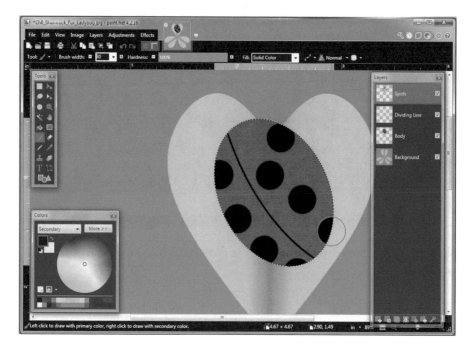

Figure 9-26. *Use the Paintbrush Tool to apply spots to the body*

21.   Deactivate the selection (Edit ➤ Deselect).

22.   Add a new layer (Layers ➤ Add New Layer).

23.   Double-click the new layer's preview thumbnail to launch the
Layer Properties dialog; rename the layer *Head* or something
similar, then click OK.

24.   Using the *Shapes Tool* (with the *Draw/Fill* mode selected), draw
an ellipse and rotate it as shown in Figure 9-27.

Figure 9-27. *Use the Shapes Tool to draw an ellipse and rotate it as shown*

25. Click the layer's (named *Body*) preview thumbnail to make it active.

26. Using the *Magic Wand Tool* (S,S,S,S), click the red ellipse to select the outline.

27. Invert the selection (Edit ➤ Invert Selection).

28. Click the layer named *Head* to make it active.

29. Erase the selection (Edit ➤ Erase Selection); this action will only remove the pixels outside of the ellipse (Figure 9-28).

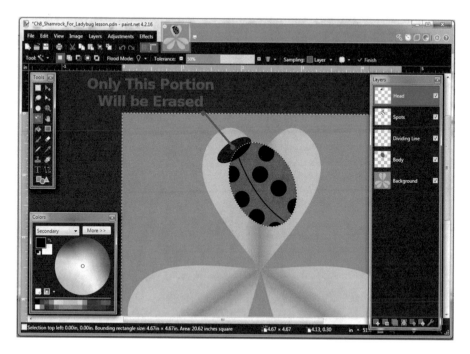

Figure 9-28. *Erase the selection to remove the excess part of the area shown*

30. Deactivate the selection (Edit ➤ Deselect).

31. Using the *Paintbrush Tool* (B) with the *Brush width* set to 57 and the *hardness* set to 100%, click on the area shown to complete the head (Figure 9-29).

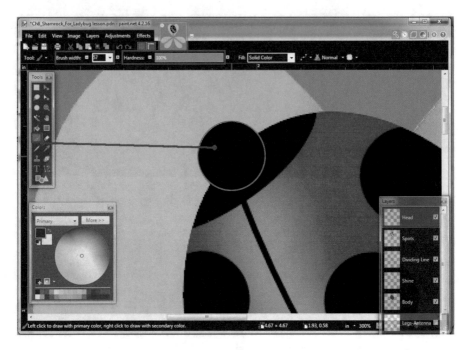

Figure 9-29. *Use the Paintbrush Tool to complete the ladybug's head*

32. In the *Colors Window*, switch the *Primary Color* to white.

33. Using the *Magic Wand Tool* (S,S,S,S), click inside the head to select it.

34. Use the *Paintbrush Tool* (B) to make two dabs as shown in Figure 9-30 within the selected area.

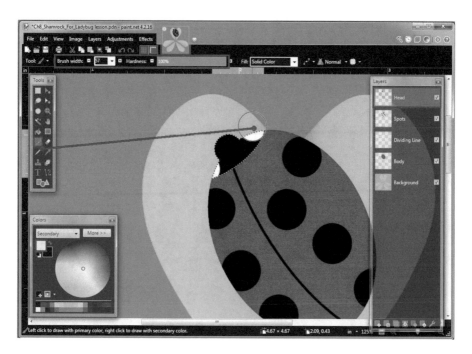

Figure 9-30. *Use the Paintbrush Tool to make two white dabs as shown*

35. Add a new layer (Layers ➤ Add New Layer).

36. Double-click the new layer's preview thumbnail to launch the Layer Properties dialog; rename the layer *Legs-Antenna*, or something similar, then click OK.

37. In the *Colors Window*, set the *Primary Color* to black.

38. Using the *Line/Curve Tool* (set to *Bezier* mode), draw the antenna (5 pixels wide) and the legs (10 pixels wide) as shown in Figure 9-31; use the Control Nodes to bend each one before drawing the next one.

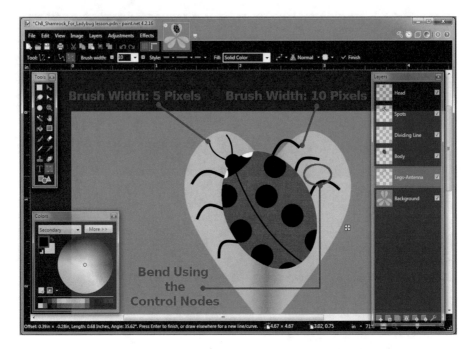

Figure 9-31. *Use the Line/Curve Tool to draw the antenna and legs as shown*

39. Add a new layer (Layers ➤ Add New Layer)—place it between the layers named *Body* and *Dividing Line*.

40. Double-click the new layer's preview thumbnail to launch the Layer Properties dialog; rename the layer *Shine*, or something similar, then click OK.

41. In the *Colors Window*, set the *Primary Color* to white.

42. Paint along the length of the ladybug's body as shown in Figure 9-32.

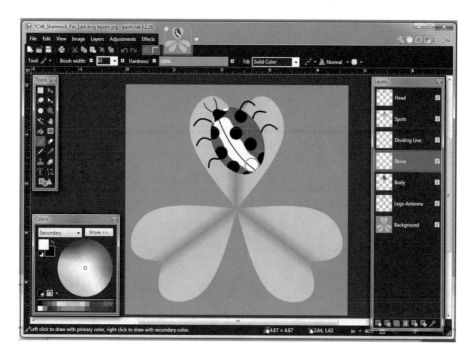

Figure 9-32. *Paint along the length of the ladybug's body as shown*

43. Open the Gaussian Blur dialog (Effects ➤ Blurs ➤ Gaussian
     Blur), and adjust the Radius to about 50, then click OK
     (Figure 9-33).

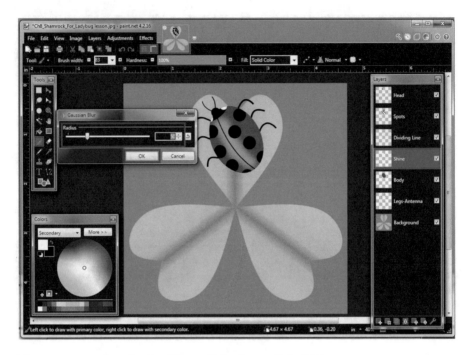

Figure 9-33. *Set the Radius to 50, then click OK*

The final result should look something like the example in Figure 9-34—
it may not be exactly as shown, of course, but that's okay. When done, save
the work as a pdn file (Paint.NET's native file format) or close it out.

Figure 9-34. *The final result*

Chapter Conclusion

We covered a lot in this chapter. As we can see, Paint.NET offers a decent array of tools and features for creating digital artwork from scratch.

Here's a recap of what was covered:

- Drawing a basic sketch

- Drawing a shamrock

- Drawing a ladybug (combined with the shamrock drawing)

In the next chapter, we'll learn about filters to apply artistic effects to photos.

CHAPTER 10

Applying Effects

In this final chapter, we'll finish things by enjoying a few fun and easy tutorials—in this case by applying effects to enhance photos or turn them into digital art.

The topics and tutorials covered in this chapter are

- Tutorial 27: Applying a Dream Effect (Dream Plugin Required)

- Tutorial 28: Applying an Ink Sketch Effect

- Tutorial 29: Applying an Oil Painting Effect (Oil Painting + Plugin Required)

- Tutorial 30: Applying a Pastel Effect (Pastel Plugin Required)

- Tutorial 31: Applying a Pencil Sketch Effect

- Chapter Conclusion

TUTORIAL 27: APPLYING A DREAM EFFECT (DREAM PLUGIN REQUIRED)

In this tutorial, we're going to give an image a dreamlike effect using the Hue/Saturation Adjustment and BoltBait's Dream Plugin:

1. Open the practice image *Ch10_Dream_Effect* in Paint.NET.

2. Duplicate the Background layer by clicking the Duplicate Layer tab at the bottom of the Layers Window.

3. Rename the layer *Dream*, or something similar.

4. Open the *Hue/Saturation dialog* (Adjustments ➤ Hue/
    Saturation)—if necessary, click Reset to restore the dialog to
    the default settings.

5. Increase the saturation level to 135, then click OK (Figure 10-1).

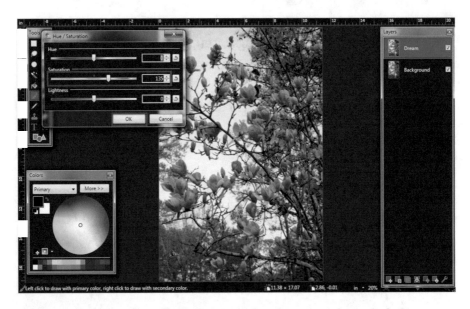

Figure 10-1. *Increase the saturation level to 135, then click OK*

6. We'll now give the image a soft dreamlike appearance—open
    the *Dream plugin dialog* (Effects ➤ Artistic ➤ Dream).

7. Lower the Focus slider to 25, then click OK (Figure 10-2).

Figure 10-2. *Lower the focus level to 25, then click OK*

By boosting the saturation and applying the Dream effect, the image has a vibrant, surreal quality (Figure 10-3). When done, save the work as a pdn file (Paint.NET's native file format) or close it out.

Figure 10-3. *The before and after comparison*

TUTORIAL 28: APPLYING AN INK SKETCH EFFECT

In this tutorial, we're going to apply an effect turning a photograph into a digital ink sketch:

1. Open the practice image *Ch10_Ink_Sketch* in Paint.NET.

2. Duplicate the Background layer by clicking the Duplicate Layer tab at the bottom of the Layers Window.

3. Rename the layer *Ink Sketch*, or something similar.

4. Open the *Ink Sketch dialog* (Effects ➤ Artistic ➤ Ink Sketch)— if necessary, click Reset to restore the dialog to the default settings.

5. Move the Ink Outline slider to 65 and the Coloring slider to 0,
    then click OK (Figure 10-4).

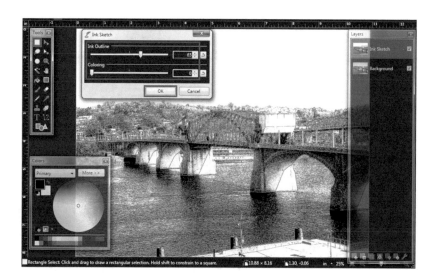

Figure 10-4. *Set the Ink Outline to 65 and the Coloring to 0, then click OK*

By applying this effect, the image now looks like a reasonable facsimile of an ink sketch (Figure 10-5). When done, save the work as a pdn file (Paint.NET's native file format) or close it out.

Figure 10-5. *The before and after comparison*

If desired, you can leave some color when using the Ink Sketch Effect as seen in Figure 10-6.

Figure 10-6. *Applying the Ink Sketch Effect with the Coloring slider set to 30*

TUTORIAL 29: APPLYING AN OIL PAINTING EFFECT (OIL PAINTING + PLUGIN REQUIRED)

In this tutorial, we're going to convert a photo into a digital oil painting by applying BoltBait's Oil Painting + plugin and the Posterize Adjustment:

1. Open the practice image *Ch10_Oil_Painting* in Paint.NET.

2. Duplicate the Background layer by clicking the Duplicate Layer tab at the bottom of the Layers Window.

3. Rename the layer *Oil Painting*, or something similar.

4. Open the *Oil Painting + dialog* (Effects ➤ Artistic ➤ Oil Painting +)—if necessary, click Reset to restore the dialog to the default settings.

5. Move the Shadow Amount and Brush Size sliders to 10 and the Shadow Detail slider to 1, then click OK (Figure 10-7).

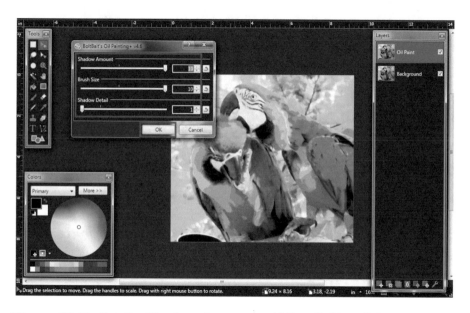

Figure 10-7. *Set the Shadow Amount and Brush Size sliders to 10 and the Shadow Detail slider to 1, then click OK*

6. Open the *Posterize Adjustment dialog* (Adjustments ➤ Posterize).

7. Make sure the Linked box is checked, move the red, green, and blue sliders simultaneously to 5, then click OK (Figure 10-8).

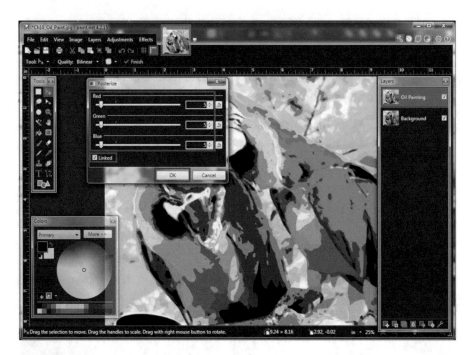

Figure 10-8. *Move the sliders to 5, then click OK.*

The image now has a painted look—note the example on the far right of Figure 10-9. When done, save the work as a pdn file (Paint.NET's native file format) or close it out.

Figure 10-9. *The before and after comparison*

TUTORIAL 30: APPLYING A PASTEL EFFECT (PASTEL PLUGIN REQUIRED)

In this lesson, we'll use BoltBait's Pastel to give a photo a "pastel drawn" look:

1. Open the practice image *Ch10_Pastel_Flower* in Paint.NET.

2. Duplicate the Background layer by clicking the Duplicate Layer tab at the bottom of the Layers Window.

3. Double-click the duplicate layer's preview thumbnail to launch the Layer Properties dialog; rename the layer *Pastel*, or something similar—then click OK.

4. Launch the *Pastel Plugin dialog* (Effects ➤ Artistic ➤ Pastel).

5. Move the *Pastel Size* slider to 8 and the *Roughness* slider to 50, then click OK (Figure 10-10).

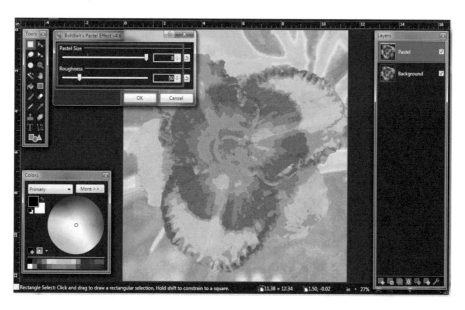

Figure 10-10. *Move the Pastel Size slider to 8 and the Roughness slider to 50, then click OK*

The image now resembles artwork rendered in pastels (Figure 10-11). When done, save the work as a pdn file (Paint.NET's native file format) or close it out.

Figure 10-11. *The before and after comparison*

TUTORIAL 31: APPLYING A PENCIL SKETCH EFFECT

In this last tutorial, we'll convert a photograph into a digital pencil sketch. This effect basically works by detecting the edges in the image and simulating a pencil outline:

1. Open the practice image *Ch10_Pencil_Sketch* in Paint.NET.

2. Duplicate the Background layer by clicking the Duplicate Layer tab at the bottom of the Layers Window.

3. Double-click the duplicate layer's preview thumbnail to launch the Layer Properties dialog; rename the layer *Sketch*, or something similar—then click OK.

4. Launch the *Pencil Sketch dialog* (Effects ➤ Artistic ➤ Pencil Sketch).

5. Move the *Pencil tip size* slider to 10 and the *Range* slider to 5, then click OK (Figure 10-12).

Figure 10-12. *Move the Pencil tip size slider to 10 and the Range slider to 5, then click OK*

The image now resembles artwork rendered as a sketch (Figure 10-13). When done, save the work as a pdn file (Paint.NET's native file format) or close it out.

Figure 10-13. *The before and after comparison*

By setting the sliders to their maximum values, the result will show more detail (Figure 10-14).

Figure 10-14. *Setting the sliders to their maximum values increase the detail in the image*

Chapter Conclusion

Well, we've finally reached the end and covered a wide range of editing lessons. By now, you undoubtedly have a good understanding of this lightweight yet capable image editor.

Here's a recap of what was covered:

- Applying a Dream Effect

- Applying an Ink Sketch Effect

- Applying an Oil Painting Effect

- Applying a Pastel Effect

- Applying a Pencil Sketch Effect

If you're ready to learn some additional plugins for Paint.NET, be sure to refer to the Appendix. I hope you found this book useful and enjoy using Paint.NET!

More About Paint.NET Plugins

One of the advantages of working with Paint.NET is that it is a nice, slim image editing program ideal for beginners. As one's proficiency grows, the program's capabilities can be expanded by adding plugins.

The BoltBait Plugin Pack (the installation was covered in Chapter 1) adds a lot of functionality to Paint.NET. In this part of the book, we'll look at some additional plugins that will add more functionality, making Paint. NET even more powerful. These particular plugins are some of the ones that I find especially useful.

Note Plugins are created by a wide variety of people active in the Paint.NET community. When looking for plugins, the recommended source is from the Paint.NET Plugin Index page found here: `https:// forums.getpaint.net/forum/7-plugins-publishing-only/`.

Null54 Content Aware

Content aware replaces the area within a selection with surrounding pixels; this aids in digitally "removing" objects.

© Phillip Whitt 2022
P. Whitt, *Practical Paint.NET*, https://doi.org/10.1007/978-1-4842-7283-1

- Download link: `https://github.com/0xC0000054/`
  `pdn-content-aware-fill/releases/download/`
  `v1.4.3/ContentAwareFill.zip`

- How to install (from the "Read Me" page included with
  the plugin download):

  1. Exit Paint.NET.

  2. Place *ContentAwareFill.dll* in the Paint.NET
      Effects folder which is usually located in one of
      the following locations depending on the Paint.
      NET version you have installed:

      Classic: C:\Program Files\Paint.NET\Effects

      Microsoft Store: My Documents\paint.net App
      Files\Effects

  3. Restart Paint.NET.

  4. The plugin will now be available as the Content
      Aware Fill menu item in the Selection category
      of the Paint.NET Effects menu (Figure A-1).

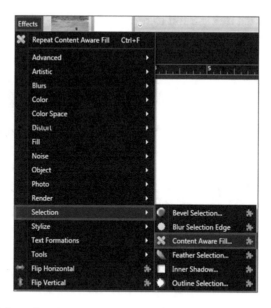

Figure A-1. *After the Content Aware plugin is installed, it can be found in Effects (Effects ➤ Selection ➤ Content Aware Fill)*

This is a useful tool that can save a lot of time and work when digitally removing objects. It works best in images with large areas of content such as bodies of water, grass, sky, etc.

The dialog offers these options:

- Sample Area Size (in pixels)

- Sample From (all around, sides, or top and bottom)

- Fill Direction (random, inward toward center, or outward from center)

- Render automatically (when the box is ticked, the action is applied without clicking the OK button)

In Figure A-2, it's being used to remove a sewer drain cover in a grassy area.

Figure A-2. *The Content Aware Fill being used to digitally remove a sewer drain cover*

In Figure A-3, we can see the result; this action was carried out in a few seconds, but using the Clone Stamp Tool would have taken much longer.

Figure A-3. *The sewer drain cover was quickly removed using the Content Aware Fill plugin*

TR's Dodge/Burn

The Dodge and Burn tools are used to lighten and darken specific areas of an image.

- Download link: `https://forums.getpaint.net/applications/core/interface/file/attachment.php?id=10070`

- Video overview: `https://youtu.be/0di9LUwXSIw`

- How to install:

  1. Exit Paint.NET.

  2. Place *TRs DodgeBurn.dll* and *TRs DodgeBurn. resources.dll* in the Paint.NET Effects folder which is usually located in one of the following locations depending on the Paint.NET version you have installed:

     Classic: C:\Program Files\Paint.NET\Effects

     Microsoft Store: My Documents\paint.net App Files\Effects

  3. Restart Paint.NET.

  4. The plugin will now be available as the TR's Dodge and Burn menu item in the Photo category of the Paint.NET Effects menu (Figure A-4).

Figure A-4. *After TR's Dodge and Burn plugin is installed, it can be found in Effects (Effects ➤ Photo ➤ TR's Dodge and Burn)*

TR's (TechnoRobbo's) Dodge and Burn plugin is a very useful dialog that adds a lot of editing power to Paint.NET. It allows you to lighten or darken specific areas in your image. In Figure A-5, the Dodge tool is being used to lighten the fur on the cat (the Burn tool has the opposite effect and darkens).

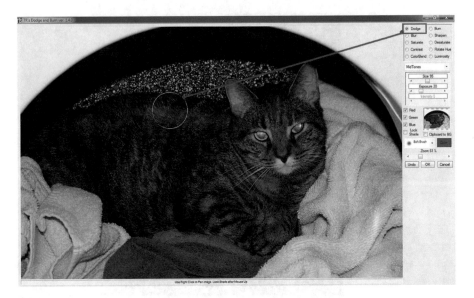

Figure A-5.   *The Dodge tool is being used to lighten the cat's fur*

In addition to lightening and darkening, this plugin allows you to apply the following effects selectively:

- Blur

- Sharpen

- Saturate

- Desaturate

- Contrast

- Rotate Hue

- ColorBlend

- Luminosity

TR's Portrait Retouch

This plugin helps soften and smooth the look of the skin in portraits, selfies, etc.

- Download link: https://forums.getpaint.net/
  applications/core/interface/file/attachment.
  php?id=9091

- How to install:

  1. Exit Paint.NET.

  2. Place *TRs Retouch.dll* in the Paint.NET Effects folder which is usually located in one of the following locations depending on the Paint. NET version you have installed:

     Classic: C:\Program Files\Paint.NET\Effects

     Microsoft Store: My Documents\paint.net App Files\Effects

  3. Restart Paint.NET.

  4. The plugin will now be available as the TR's Portrait Retouch menu item in the Photo category of the Paint.NET Effects menu (Figure A-6).

Figure A-6. *After TR's Portrait Retouch plugin is installed, it can be found in Effects (Effects ➤ Photo ➤ TR's Portrait Retouch)*

TR's (TechnoRobbo's) Portrait Retouch plugin is another useful dialog that allows you to give portraits a soft, smooth look. As Figure A-7 shows, the areas I wanted to apply the effect to have been selected. The dialog allows you to control the amount of the effect, diffusion, brightness, and to reduce detail.

Figure A-7. *TR's Portrait Retouch dialog allows you to control the amount of the effect, the diffusion, brightness, and reduce detail*

Figure A-8 shows the before and after comparison.

Figure A-8. *The before and after comparison*

PSD Plugin for Paint.NET

This allows files to be saved or open images in Adobe Photoshop's .psd file format.

- Download link: www.psdplugin.com/files/
  PSDPlugin-2.5.0.zip

- How to install (as instructed by the plugin provider's website):

  (Make sure you have the latest version of Paint.NET installed—check this in Help-About.)

  1. Close Paint.NET.

  2. Download and open the ZIP file.

3. Copy and paste PhotoShop.dll to C:\Program
    Files\paint.net\FileTypes.

    • The Windows Store version of Paint.NET uses
       different plugin directories. See the Paint.NET
       documentation, in the yellow box that says "In
       the Windows Store version of paint.net": www.
       getpaint.net/doc/latest/InstallPlugins.html.

4. Restart Paint.NET, which will automatically
    detect the PSD file type plugin (Figure A-9).

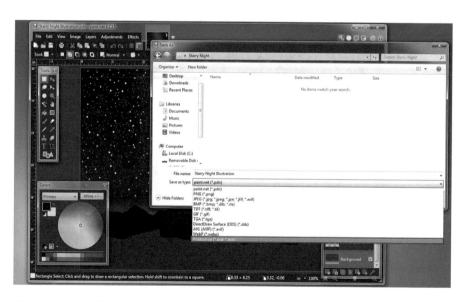

Figure A-9. *The PSD plugin for Paint.NET is automatically detected after being installed*

This plugin (provided by www.psdplugin.com/) allows you to save or open your work in the psd file format used by Adobe Photoshop (as well as GIMP, PaintShop Pro, and other programs). Figure A-10 shows a layered image that was first created in Paint.NET, then converted into a .psd file, which is now opened in Adobe Photoshop.

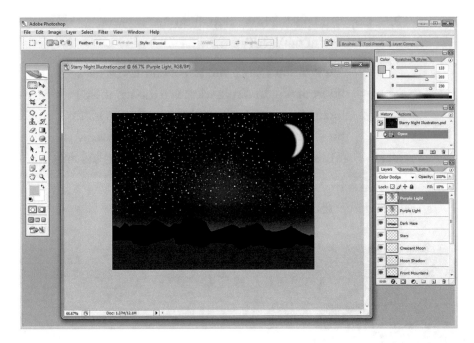

Figure A-10. *This image was originally created in Paint.NET and converted into a .psd file, which is now opened in Adobe Photoshop*

Note   In some cases, there will only be partial compatibility between programs. For example, adjustment layers created in Photoshop generally do not function when opened in Paint.NET (they open as empty layers). Layer blend modes may behave differently between programs as well. This plugin works best when working with images containing raster layers set to the Normal blend mode.

G'MIC-Qt

This dialog offers a wide variety of filters for artistic and photographic effects.

- Download links:

  - (32-bit version) `https://github.com/0xC0000054/pdn-gmic/releases/download/v2.9.7/Gmic_win32.zip`

  - (64-bit version) `https://github.com/0xC0000054/pdn-gmic/releases/download/v2.9.7/Gmic_win64.zip`

- How to install (from the "Read Me" page included with the plugin download):

  1. Close Paint.NET.

  2. Place Gmic.dll and the gmic folder in the Paint.NET Effects folder which is usually located in one of the following locations depending on the Paint.NET version you have installed:

     Classic: C:\Program Files\Paint.NET\Effects

     Microsoft Store: Documents\paint.net App Files\Effects

  3. Restart Paint.NET.

  4. The plugin will now be available as the G'MIC-Qt menu item in the Advanced category of the Paint.NET Effects menu (Figure A-11).

Figure A-11. *After the G'MIC-Qt plugin is installed, it can be found in Effects (Effects ➤ Advanced ➤ G'MIC-Qt)*

(Make sure you have the latest version of Paint.NET installed—check this in Help-About.)

G'MIC-Qt (GREYC's Magic for Image Computing) is an open source framework available for several programs such as GIMP, Krita, Photoshop, PaintShop Pro, and a few others. This plugin offers a large variety of filters for artistic and photographic effects.

In Figure A-12, the Cartoon filter is applied to the image in the preview window.

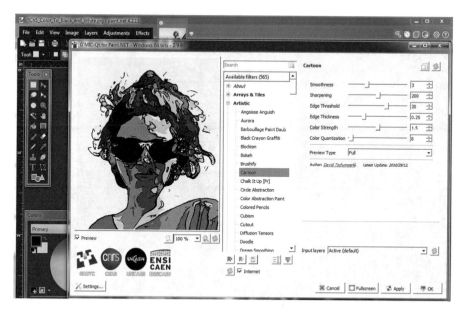

Figure A-12. *The Cartoon filter is applied to the image in the preview window*

Another example is the Black and White dialog used to convert images from color to black and white. Back in Chapter 5 (Tutorial 11), we used BoltBait's Black and White + plugin to convert this color image. It offers a few control sliders and presets to let you adjust the result. In Figure A-13, we can see the Black and White dialog in the G'MIC-Qt plugin offers a wide array of adjustments to achieve the best possible result.

Figure A-13. *The Black and White dialog offers a wide array of adjustments for achieving the best possible result*

For more information about G'MIC-Qt, visit http://gmic.eu/index.html.

Brush Factory V2.0

This plugin offers a variety of dynamic brushes with customized shapes.

- How to download: Follow the link here—https://
  drive.google.com/open?id=0B6r81tGW7hODS1hvODZR
  NGpyUWs.

  Google Drive will open, then the Brush Factory
  zip file can be acquired by clicking the Download
  button (Figure A-14).

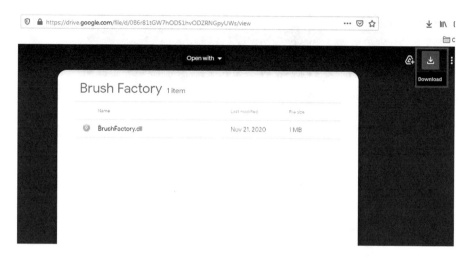

Figure A-14. *After Google Drive opens, the Brush Factory zip file can be downloaded*

- How to install:

  1. Close Paint.NET.

  2. Place BrushFactory.dll in the Paint.NET Effects folder which is usually located in one of the following locations depending on the Paint. NET version you have installed:

     Classic: C:\Program Files\Paint.NET\Effects

     Microsoft Store: Documents\paint.net App Files\Effects

  3. Restart Paint.NET.

  4. The plugin will now be available as the Brush Factory menu item in the Tools category of the Paint.NET Effects menu (Figure A-15).

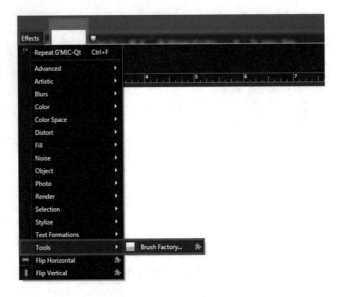

Figure A-15. *After the Brush Factory plugin is installed, it can be found in Effects (Effects ➤ Tools ➤ Brush Factory)*

Brush Factory (by Joshua Lamusga) offers customization dynamic brushes for creating shapes such as grass, smoke, dirt, and others. Figure A-16 shows the Segments brush.

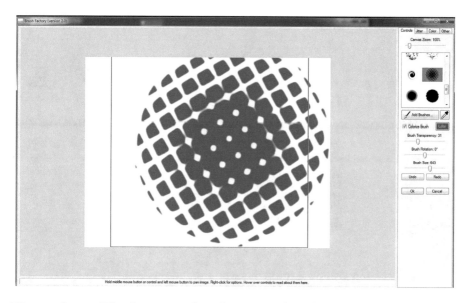

Figure A-16. *The Segments brush is one of the brushes found in the Brush Factory menu*

In the following example, the illustration of the camera (Figure A-17) was created using Paint.NET, and the flash was added by using the Spark brush in Brush Factory (the brush transparency was increased by 20%).

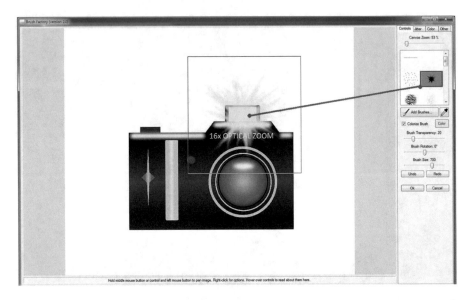

Figure A-17. *The camera illustration was created in Paint.NET, and the flash added using the Spark brush in the Brush Factory dialog*

For more information on using the Brush Factory, visit:

`https://github.com/JoshuaLamusga/Brush-Factory/wiki/How-to-Use-Brush-Factory`

Conclusion

These are just some of the many plugins available for Paint.NET, and it's easy to see how they can really boost the power of this program. To see more plugins, visit the Plugin Index here: `https://forums.getpaint.net/forum/7-plugins-publishing-only/`.

Index

P, Q

R

S

Printed in the United States
by Baker & Taylor Publisher Services